Political Realism
in American Thought

POLITICAL REALISM
IN AMERICAN THOUGHT

John W. Coffey

LEWISBURG
BUCKNELL UNIVERSITY PRESS
LONDON: ASSOCIATED UNIVERSITY PRESSES

© 1977 by Associated University Presses, Inc.

Associated University Presses, Inc.
Cranbury, New Jersey 08512

Associated University Presses
Magdalen House
136-148 Tooley Street
London SE1 2TT, England

Library of Congress Cataloging in Publication Data

Coffey, John W.   1943-
    Political realism in American thought.

    Bibliography: p.
    Includes index.
    1.   Political science—United States—History.
2.   Realism.   I.   Title.
JA84.U5C58   320.5   76-760
ISBN 08387-1903-1

The author wishes to thank Little, Brown and Company for permission to reprint selections from George F. Kennan, *Memoirs: 1925–1950*, copyright © 1967 by George F. Kennan, and from his *Memoirs: 1950–1963*, Volume II, copyright © 1972 by George F. Kennan. Quoted by permission of Little, Brown and Co., in association with The Atlantic Monthly Press.

PRINTED IN THE UNITED STATES OF AMERICA

For Margaret

CONTENTS

PREFACE

These pages constitute an essay on aspects of modern American political thought. The present study in intellectual history treats what the philosopher Jacques Maritain, using an old scholastic description, called "practical philosophy." [1] Practical philosophy is neither wholly speculative nor wholly instrumental in nature; rather, it is a mode of knowledge that remains speculative in essence but that is directed toward action as its object. Although as a historian I am aware of treading on dangerous ground by entering the domain of politics, the sense that political theory is too important to be left solely to either political scientists or professional philosophers emboldens me to forge ahead. Whatever the merits of my effort, the reader will perhaps forgive a historian's temerity in approaching political theory, recalling that the endeavor itself has noble precedent in the writings of the ancient historians. It is my intention to bring a sense of history to our political experience, but I am not, the reader will discover, a historicist.

In these essays I have set out to assess the meaning of realism as a political philosophy. *Realism* is not a univocal concept. It does not connote the same thing to each of its proponents, and from time to time its implications change for particular thinkers. Nevertheless, since about the 1930s American political thought has been markedly influenced by one variety or another of a doctrine known as realism. My interpretation of the dominant political philosophy in America during the last generation focuses upon three of its principal advocates: the Protestant theologian Reinhold Niebuhr, the diplomat-historian George Kennan, and the political theorist Hans Morgenthau.

While he was a radical socialist in the 1930s, Niebuhr formulated the doctrine of Christian realism as an alternative to both the reliance of the Protestant social gospel upon moral suasion and the faith of secular liberalism in the meliorative effects of scientific reason. After World War II he became the chief spokesman for a chastened, more hardheaded liberalism. A political analyst and participant in organizations such as the Americans for Democratic Action, Niebuhr defended the New Deal welfare-state achievements against socialist and conservative critics alike and supplied a theological justification for America's cold war foreign policy. For more than twenty years Christian realism informed the outlook of a wide spectrum of intellectuals. Few individuals exerted a greater impact on modern liberalism than Reinhold Niebuhr, the man who, George Kennan once declared, was "the father of us all."

In his capacity as head of the important Policy Planning Staff at the State Department in 1947, George Kennan was a major architect of the policy of containment in American statecraft. Leaving the State Department shortly thereafter, Kennan added to his public service an illustrious career as a student of American diplomacy, during which he enunciated the foreign policy of disengagement and provided searching insight into the general political life of the nation.

For many years the renowned scholar of politics and diplomacy at the University of Chicago, Hans Morgenthau has elaborated a comprehensive doctrine of realism in those fields. Morgenthau is a more strictly academic figure than Niebuhr or Kennan, but he has been an influential exponent of the principles of national self-interest and the balance of power in international relations. Among his other achievements, Morgenthau has upheld the primacy of theory in the science of international relations, and it is with his fundamental theory of politics that I shall be concerned.

Chapter 1 deals with George Kennan's character and view of man and society in light of certain realist principles that he postulates; the second chapter treats Kennan's foreign-policy position and his analysis of the relation between power, self-interest, and morality in diplomacy. Chapter 3 traces the development of Niebuhr's Christian realism from his radical socialist stance during the 1930s through his later liberal, pragmatist stage. The last chapter offers an explication and evaluation of the philosophical foundation of Morgenthau's political realism. I am not concerned with Niebuhr's formal theology as such, and neither in his case nor in Kennan's am I directly interested in the origins of and responsibility for the cold war. These matters have been written about elsewhere and at length; the second, moreover, belongs to a different kind of historical study. Insofar as my discussion entails a review of domestic political issues and specific foreign policies, it does so in order to establish a context within which to examine the concept of realism. My purpose is to see what realism means as a way of looking at political problems, as a canon, in other words, of political thought. I have criticisms to make of the doctrine of realism as it is construed by each writer, but despite these criticisms, I wish to affirm my respect for all three men. It is a compliment to a person to take him seriously enough to criticize him, and in this spirit I offer my remarks.

Briefly, my contention is that Niebuhr's Christian realism differs little from the secular, liberal pragmatism that he repudiated. I thus think that Morton White in his book *Social Thought in America: The Revolt against Formalism* is misled in his estimate of Niebuhr. White regards Niebuhr's Christian realism as an obscurantist atavism, a lamentable relapse from America's basically sound liberal pragmatic tradition. He should, on the contrary, perceive how close Niebuhr is to that tradition. But I shall return to this point in the epilogue. Kennan's realism, I believe, is inconsistent with his own deepest character and personal vision, and his realism fails to explain adequately his views on foreign policy. Realism, furthermore, does not obviate the intrusion of moralism into the conduct of foreign relations, nor does moralism inhibit the pursuit of national self-interest. Morgenthau's philosophically more articulate theory of political realism unites certain premises of both Niebuhr's and Kennan's concepts, and in Morgenthau's doctrine can be seen the radical, disintegrative tendency of the modern spirit.

It might be noted that in recent years all three men altered their views on foreign policy, although I have not felt it necessary for my intention to consider current events. Niebuhr, Kennan, and Morgenthau eventually came to oppose the Vietnam War; yet I have deliberately chosen to avoid this issue. Doubtless, some people will disagree, but I believe that discussion of Vietnam cannot yet appreciably rise above the level of journalism. Vietnam is simply too nearly contemporaneous for us to have sufficient perspective on it. At best, we can entertain opinions about it, though of course these opinions may be more or less informed. I suspect the vigor of dissent from my position testifies to the prematurity of the issue. Serious problems must be allowed to season a bit before one can satisfactorily deal with them. At any rate, the subject of this study is political realism, not an intellectual history of the cold war. Toward this end I have for the most part restricted myself to a period roughly from the middle 1930s to the late 1950s, referring to particular controversies only for illustrative purposes.

Inevitably, however, my assessment of these men's responses to foreign affairs rests partially upon the overall interpretation of the cold war that I hold, so it is appropriate at this point to present summarily my views on that subject. Sufficient time has elapsed, I think, to advance some tentative judgments about the origins of and responsibility for the cold war, especially as these questions bear upon deeper issues of political reality and historical causation. It is at this level that various historiographical schools ultimately differ; thus, for the reader unfamiliar with the scholarly debate over the cold war, it might be useful to outline the major rival interpretations, indicating my own position along the way.

In addition to the men in this book, Arthur M. Schlesinger, Jr., among others, has stated the conventional liberal-realist view of the cold war. According to Schlesinger, Soviet ideological dogmatism and Stalin's paranoia made the cold war unavoidable. Both the American desire for an Open Door in the world and political pressure at home from ethnic groups set us against Stalin's spheres-of-influence policy. Russia, however, was no traditional nation-state, and although at times America succumbed to self-righteousness, the inherent pseudo-religious nature of Communism transformed the political conflict into a "religious war." Thus, concludes Schlesinger, "the most rational of American policies could hardly have averted the Cold War." [2]

This account of American innocence in foreign affairs has been challenged in recent years by younger historians of a leftist persuasion. [3] These revisionists, though they differ on a number of secondary points, commonly maintain that Russia was a conservative national state that wanted a spheres-of-influence policy for legitimate economic and strategic reasons. The United States' commitment to the Open Door, then,

generated a cold war for which she bears principal responsibility. Specifically, the foreign policy of the Open Door was
dictated by a capitalist economy requiring overseas markets,
raw materials, and investment sources. Hence the United States
deliberately and systematically pursued a hegemonic position
in an integrated world market in order to save capitalism at
home and abroad. At least from 1945 to 1946, if not before, the
United States abandoned a policy of negotiation and accom-
modation, since economic pressure and even atomic intimida-
tion failed to thwart Stalin's limited purpose.

John Gaddis's study of the early years of the cold war adopts
an intermediate position between the orthodox and revisionist
interpretations. [4] Gaddis does not deny that the needs of a
capitalist economy required an Open Door abroad and the
containment of Communism, but he reasonably suggests that
the economic determination of policy-making is too narrow. He
shows how domestic political pressure from ethnic groups and
various voting blocs severely hampered American policy-
makers, and he rightly observes that a theory of economic
determinism deprives leftist critics of any basis for assigning
moral responsibility to America. It might be added that the
moral censure delivered by revisionists is a philosophical rather
than historical judgment, and scholarly debate would be
considerably clarified if this were explicitly acknowledged.
Gaddis concludes that while neither Russia nor America was
entirely responsible for the cold war, the conflict was not
inevitable either; in his view the final blame lies with Russia,
because as a dictator Stalin had more flexibility in policy-making than democratic statesmen. Yet Gaddis seems to forget that
America was far stronger than Russia at the end of World War
II, and he admits that Russia did not initially communize her
occupied countries and that Stalin did not always support
foreign Communist parties.

The most serious critique of radical historiography has been offered by Robert Tucker in a thin but weighty book, *The Radical Left and American Foreign Policy*. Tucker grants much truth to the radical position, praising it for demonstrating the "obsessive self-interest" of American foreign policy and for introducing a note of realism absent in the orthodox interpretation. Actually, the radical thesis is startling, Tucker claims, only when compared to conventional historiography. Revisionists correctly see too that American policy, far from floundering on illusion and error as the liberal-realist argument holds, has deliberately aimed at global hegemony and that, indeed, the Open Door has constituted the heart of American strategy in the twentieth century.

Nevertheless, Tucker contends, the United States has acted no differently from the way that great powers have always acted. Never denying that America sought a postwar equilibrium favorable to her, one facet of which was the strengthening of capitalism, Tucker subjects the materialist reductionism and determinism of the radical position to a penetrating criticism, arguing instead that a real but exaggerated American need for security made the cold war inevitable. This justifiable desire for security found expression in the early policy of containment, but fatefully the Truman Doctrine harbored a false and inflated notion of security that eventually distorted American policy. Tucker is right that radicals typically fail to appreciate "the deeper sources of collective self-aggrandizement"[5] and that the history of diplomacy shows that expansion is not dependent upon a particular socioeconomic structure, for states always identify themselves with a larger meaning and purpose. A good example of Tucker's point would be the Peloponnesian War in which the Athenians too sought a favorable equilibrium of power, one aspect of which was its economic benefit. Historians should never overlook the economic factor in politics, but the assertion of its exclusive dominance is a philosophical rather than historical claim. Power per se, not particular forms of it, maintains Tucker, causes expansion; moreover, radicals fail to prove that even with socialist institutions we would act differently, or that there would be no real threats to us.

The central revisionist theses concerning East Europe, America's use of the atomic bomb, and the alleged quest for capitalist world hegemony have been scrutinized by Charles Maier.[6] Maier also concedes a portion of the radical case on these issues, but he illustrates how that case is not quite so simple and offers additional considerations. With ample warrant he charges that much revisionist thinking has been skewed by the impact of Vietnam and the attempt to read back into history subsequent problems with the Third World.

The basic issue in cold war historiography, Maier correctly emphasizes, is a philosophical and methodological one; that is, only certain kinds of explanation for international politics and foreign-policy formation are acceptable to revisionists. Though I see no reason to think revisionists alone are guilty of this, Maier fairly says that they tend to ignore elements such as the intrinsic tension in international affairs, domestic opinion, and physical security. For his part Maier stresses the importance of bureaucracy in shaping foreign policy through its efforts to justify itself and exert its influence. He gives some useful examples of this influence, and he is certainly right that those who accentuate the bureaucratic process are asking different kinds of historical questions from those of the people who do not. The former are inquiring *how* a policy is formed, not *why*, but it does not follow that the revisionist concern with *why* imposes extra-historical values on the meaning of policies. Why the Civil War happened or why the feudal system collapsed is a legitimate historical question, though one may make an extra-historical judgment about those developments. Maier mistakes the problem, I think, but it is a significant problem, one that deserves to be aired. The danger with his attention to process in history is that it tends to dissolve responsibility and finally to remove the human dimension from history altogether. Orthodox as well as revisionist writers make nonhistorical judgments about liberal-capitalist institutions, and this philosophical debate should be made explicit. If, however, a revisionist or anyone else deals inadequately with the evidence in questions of historical explanation and causation, that is simply bad history, not nonhistory.

In the end, then, we return to where we began, the nexus between history and political thought, or practical philosophy. Before proceeding I should perhaps advise the reader that I do not undertake this study with a spirit of scientific neutrality or spectatorial indifference, and I trust my position will be clear. I hope to be able, as David Potter once said in another context, to be detached though not uncommitted.

Acknowledgments

To Barton Bernstein, David Kennedy, and Kirk Jeffrey, who read most of these pages at one stage or another and provided valuable criticism and encouragement, I owe a deep debt of gratitude. John V. Glass, Jr., gave a portion of these pages the benefit of his acute stylistic judgment. John Rosenberg's thoughtfulness brought my manuscript to the attention of Cynthia Fell at the Bucknell University Press, and to her and Julien Yoseloff and Mrs. Mathilde E. Finch of Associated University Presses, Inc., I am grateful for kind assistance. A grant from the Mary Ashby Cheek Fund at Rockford College aided me in publication, and Dean James Sawrey at the California State University at San Jose graciously provided me with pleasant surroundings in which to put the finishing touches on my work. This book is dedicated to my lovely wife, Margaret, whose grace, wit, and charm sustained a febrile, melancholic Irish temperament and whose keen editorial eye refined my prose.

I would like to thank the following for permission to quote from copyrighted material:

West" (Jan. 16 and 23, 1943); and "Is This 'Peace in Our Time'?" (April 7, 1945).

The New American Library, Inc., for extracts from Hans Morgenthau, *Science: Servant or Master?* Copyright © 1972 by Hans J. Morgenthau. By arrangement with The New American Library, Inc., New York, N.Y.

Princeton University Press, for extracts from George F. Kennan, *From Prague after Munich: Diplomatic Papers 1938-1940*, copyright © 1968 by Princeton University Press, and from *Realities of American Foreign Policy*, also by George F. Kennan, copyright © 1954 by Princeton University Press. Reprinted by permission of Princeton University Press.

The Progressive, Inc. for extracts from George Kennan, "Speak Truth to Power—A Reply by George Kennan," reprinted by permission from *The Progressive*, 408 West Gorham Street, Madison, Wisconsin 53703. Copyright © 1955, The Progressive, Inc.

Random House, Inc., for extracts from *Basic Writings of Saint Thomas Aquinas*, edited by Anton C. Pegis, copyright © 1945 by Random House, Inc., and from Hans Morgenthau, *The Purpose of American Politics*, copyright © 1960 by Alfred A. Knopf and Random House, Inc.

Reviews in American History, for permission to reprint portions of John W. Coffey, "The Five Faces of Walter Lippmann," *Reviews in American History* 2 (December 1974): 546-52.

Charles Scribner's Sons, for extracts from Reinhold Niebuhr, *Moral Man and Immoral Society: A Study in Ethics and Politics*, copyright © 1960, and from Reinhold Niebuhr, *The Irony of American History*, copyright © 1962 by Charles Scribner's Sons.

The University of Chicago Press, for extracts from George F. Kennan, *American Diplomacy, 1900-1950*, copyright © 1951 by The University of Chicago Press; and for extracts from Hans J. Morgenthau, *Dilemmas of Politics*, copyright © 1958 by The University of Chicago Press, and Hans J. Morgenthau, *Scientific Man vs. Power Politics*, copyright © 1965, by The University of Chicago Press.

The University of Michigan Press, for extracts from *World Technology and Human Destiny*, edited by Raymond Aron, copyright © 1963 by The University of Michigan Press.

Political Realism
in American Thought

1

The Mind of the Realist

THROUGHOUT HIS DISTINGUISHED CAREER AS A DIPLOMAT AND historian, George F. Kennan has applied a concept of realism to the conduct and study of foreign relations. Although he has never articulated a systematic political philosophy, Kennan is a reflective man of affairs who has tried to correct the errors of diplomacy in a democratic society. Once described by Louis Halle as a man "in the grip of a personal vision," which "gives him the essential character of an Old Testament prophet,"[1] Kennan's personal vision has profoundly shaped his concept of statecraft. That vision, along with the portrait of his character he paints in the *Memoirs*, provides an appropriate starting point for this study.

During World War I Randolph Bourne said of the éclat with which intellectuals greeted the conflict, "This realistic boast is so loud and sonorous that one wonders whether realism is always a stern and intelligent grappling with realities."[2] One need not hold Bourne's attitude toward World War I or war generally in order to share his doubt. According to Kennan, a steadfast objectivity marks the realist approach to politics.

The ability to cut through subjective, emotional factors to the heart of things, to see the whole and see it steadily, separates realists from utopians and sentimentalists. Kennan frequently stresses his objectivity amidst a world of deluded innocents, even though early in his *Memoirs* he discloses a radical, enduring subjectivism:

> I lived, particularly in childhood but with lessening intensity right on to middle age, in a world that was peculiarly and intimately my own, scarcely to be shared with others or even made plausible to them. I habitually read special meanings into things, scenes, and places—qualities of wonder, beauty, promise, or horror—for which there was no external evidence visible, or plausible, to others. My world was peopled with mysteries, seductive hints, vague menaces, "intimations of immortality." [3]

Such intense self-consciousness and heightened sensibility, while appropriate for a man who always regarded himself an outsider—a "guest of one's time and not a member of its household" [4]—is surprising for someone who prizes his critical detachment. Again, given Kennan's disparagement of emotion in human affairs, his craving for recognition and acceptance is disconcerting, though it is understandable for a man "in a certain sense scarred for life" [5] by the early death of his mother. Like Henry Adams, Kennan has been beset throughout life with a persistent sense of inadequacy and failure. Shortly after he was invited to the Institute for Advanced Study at Princeton University, Kennan felt afflicted by a spiritual malaise, arising from the opportunity to indulge an "awareness of one's own imperfections." His self-depreciation and discouragement were mollified, however, by "a temperament too superficial, too unserious, too much the prisoner of moods, too vulnerable to enthusiasms, too buoyant under the stress of external stimuli, to remain for long depressed or reflective." [6]

Because an objective grasp of things as they are is a hallmark of the realist posture, it is dismaying to hear Kennan assert flatly, "Things are as we see them." [7] When as a young man he left Wisconsin in 1921 for college at Princeton, taking with him "tense Presbyterian anxieties," Kennan experienced the accentuated reflexiveness that comes from being an outsider. He tells us of the effect of being "an oddball on campus":

> It finally dawned on me, pondering this unhappy situation, that to be fair to oneself one had to make one's own standards, one could not just accept those of other people; there was always the possibility that those others, in the very rejection of us, had been wrong (Ibid, p. 12)

Kennan's yearning for "intimations of immortality" remained with him over the years. The favorable reception of his famous Long Telegram from Moscow in 1946 seemed momentarily to bring glory within reach. For a brief period his "official loneliness came in fact to an end (p. 295)," but Kennan's influence was short-lived, if exhilarating. The tragic isolation of the prophet was to be his fate. Writing from Russia in the autumn of 1944, he predicted his destiny:

> There will be much talk about the necessity for "understanding Russia;" but there will be no place for the American who is really willing to undertake this disturbing task. The apprehension of what is valid in the Russian world is unsettling and displeasing to the American mind. He who would undertake this apprehension will not find his satisfaction in the achievement of anything practical for his people, still less in any official or public appreciation for his efforts. The best he can look forward to is the lonely pleasure of one who stands at long last on a chilly and inhospitable mountaintop where few have been before, where few can follow, and where few will consent to believe that he has been. (Pp. 530–31)

Kennan's views of Communism and Nazism illustrate his radical subjectivity. In the *Memoirs* he offers as a litmus test of

Marxism the fact that "I could identify myself neither with the exploiter nor with the exploited (p. 7)." He claims that insofar as the Marxist conception of exploitation and class struggle bears any verisimilitude, it is attributable to a "tragic misunderstanding" in the past rather than to any real economic conflict. The Marxist theory of history may be a more or less adequate explanation of social development, but to use as the test of its validity one's personal capacity for identification can scarcely be called objective. I shall later observe additional instances where Kennan's lack of empathy affects his political and personal judgment.

Kennan interprets Communism's appeal as a subjective one fulfilling an emotional need for identity. Watching a Communist parade of shabby workers in Hamburg in 1927, he remembers being tearfully moved to recognize "the fact that this, as they saw it, was *their* day, and that they were resolved to have their word, if only in the form of their banners and their numbers (p. 22)." Communist ideology always drew Kennan's disdain for what he considered its pretentious pseudo-science, its unscrupulous opportunism, and its cruel lust for power. From the beginning he believed Soviet ideology and leaders to be the product of a profound neurosis, at one point depicting the Communist party as "a vast, collective Walter Mitty" that evinced "the characteristic symptoms of an advanced psychosis (pp. 245–46)." To this highly affective view of Marxism and Soviet Communism Kennan added an absolute, a priori repudiation of any association with Russia. President Roosevelt's establishment of formal diplomatic relations with the Soviet Union in 1933 prompted Kennan to demur: "Never—neither then nor at any later date—did I consider the Soviet Union a fit ally or associate, actual or potential, for this country (p. 57)." There were, to be sure, elements of neuroticism and genuine evil in Stalinist Russia, though Kennan's analysis of Soviet Communism is idiosyncratic, especially when compared to his perception of Nazism.

As late as 1940 Kennan insisted that Hitler was merely a German nationalist. Advising his superiors not to distinguish too sharply between Hitler and the German people in evaluating the prospects for peace, he wrote, "the man is acting in the best traditions of German nationalism (p.116)." As a political observer at the American embassy in Prague in 1939, Kennan exhibited a remarkable indifference to the objects of Nazi terror. Explaining in a letter that the Nazis had only been after those Germans and Jews engaged in anti-Nazi activity, he added that "the press has been a little inclined to exaggerate the horrors of those first two weeks of the German occupation." [8] The Nazis lacked the "spiritual power" and "political maturity" of the Catholic Church and the Hapsburg Empire, he admitted; yet there seemed to him to be little unique about the Nazis (ibid., p. 171). Although life would never be quite the same in Czechoslovakia, on the whole the Czechs were better off under the Nazis than before:

> Few will wish for the return of the many squabbling political parties, the petty-bourgeois timidity, and the shallow materialism which seems to have characterized at least the lower organs of public administration under the former regime. Czech nationalism will flourish indeed, but with it there will be a demand for greater personal responsibility and greater spiritual authority among those who pretend to lead. (P. 224)

In a summary report entitled "A Year and a Half of the Protectorate of Bohemia and Moravia," written in October 1940, Kennan maintained the Czechs were not too unfortunate and that, anyway, they were not the only ones in Europe with problems. At least they now enjoyed a more efficient government administration (pp. 238–40).

Kennan's inability to identify with either victim or oppressor led him to reject the Marxist theory of history. Just as this limited capacity for empathy skews his political judgment, so too a callous insouciance toward tangible suffering and need colors his personal disposition. He recounts an extraordinary incident that occurred during the March crisis and final occupation of Prague by the Nazis. A Jewish acquaintance had fled in terror to Kennan's house, where

> for twenty-four hours he haunted the house, a pitiful figure of horror and despair, moving uneasily around the drawingroom, smoking one cigarette after another, too unstrung to eat or think of anything but his plight. His brother and sister-in-law had committed suicide together after Munich, and he had a strong inclination to follow suit. Annelise pleaded with him at intervals throughout the coming hours not to choose this way out, not because she or I had any great optimism with respect to his chances for future happiness but partly on general Anglo-Saxon principles and partly to preserve our home from this sort of an unpleasantness. (P. 86)

This striking lack of human feeling Kennan dismisses by saying in the *Memoirs* that he "had inherited a detestation of scenes which I can only put down as a congenital weakness of the family"; [9] nevertheless, it provides an insight into his sensibility and notion of objectivity. Kennan is susceptible to extreme subjectivity in his own favor, and his objectivity operates in such selective fashion as to impair human compassion. Bourgeois preciosity, not the righteousness of an Old Testament prophet, marks George Kennan's character. For him, realistic objectivity is useful neither for discerning what the realities of the world are nor for responding to them.

In addition to objectivity, Kennan's doctrine of realism posits the primacy of means over ends in human affairs. He is not always clear and consistent in his differentiation and evaluation of these two factors; however, Kennan typically argues that life derives its significance from the way people pursue their designs rather than from the merit of those designs. The spectacle of columns of German prisoners being marched through the streets of Moscow made men's endeavors seem feckless and vain:

I recognized at that moment, that I stood temperamentally outside the passions of war—and always would. . . . But it was primarily against people's methods rather than against their objectives that indignation mounted in such moments. Objectives were normally vainglorious, unreal, extravagant, even pathetic—little likely to be realized, scarcely to be taken seriously. People had to have them, or believe they had them. It was part of their weakness as human beings. But methods were another matter. These were real. It was out of their immediate effects that the quality of life was really molded. In war as in peace I found myself concerned less with what people thought they were striving for than with the manner in which they strove for it. Whatever such an outlook implied—whether weakness of character or qualities less reprehensible (and on this question there will never, I am sure, be wide agreement)—I was never a man for causes. [10]

One wonders why Kennan was more emotionally moved by the plight of Nazi prisoners of war than by that of the hunted Jewish soul in his drawing room. Nor is the meaning of this passage on its own terms evident. If Kennan intends to condemn war, this would not be consonant with his general foreign-policy position; even so, the case, as presented, is less than compelling. Kennan's statement might evoke a sentiment or feeling in the reader, but it does not raise the issue above the level of taste. Furthermore, Kennan does not simply say that the nature of an end is partially formed by the means utilized to obtain it; he contends, rather, that life is merely the sum of its discrete parts. This position is difficult to reconcile with Kennan's professed Christian faith. The Christian may not ignore the ethical importance of means in human action, but few Christian thinkers would be content to hold that means constitute a sufficient measure of moral action or that a good life is comprised of pleasant manners, sober goals, and deliberate methods. These may win the bourgeois a tolerable fortune and reputation in the city of man, but they fall far short of the virtue necessary to gain a place in the kingdom of God. Again, when Kennan treats elsewhere the relation of legality and morality to the end of national self-interest, his defense of the ascendancy of this end tends to neglect the means used to achieve it. Finally, Kennan's exaggerated emphasis on means in life is altogether incompatible with the aimlessness of modern America he finds so baneful.

The next chapter will take up at greater length Kennan's shifting views of foreign policy during the 1950s. For the moment, though, let us note the reason behind his call for changes in American attitudes toward Russia. The Soviet objective of world revolution, Kennan was persuaded by the mid-1950s, remained fixed; despite this, their methods had moderated, and that fact was paramount. An advocate of disengagement, Kennan exhorted America to respond temperately to the problems confronting her. But he couched his reason in a conception of human conduct more bourgeois than Christian. As if the well-bred gentleman and the saint were one, Kennan asked,

> Who are we to exalt the ends above the means? As a nation bred in the Christian tradition, we should understand something of the importance of method. We, of all people, should know that it is method—not the objective—which, in the last analysis, determines the outcome." [11]

Although Kennan occasionally speaks of the "beast" in man, the ineradicable taint of evil in human nature, his idea of human nature is essentially secular. Kennan's faith is an attenuated, genteel Calvinism marked by a diffuse, haunting sense of guilt and a confusion between morality and manners. He explains the connection between sin and bad taste thus:

> It is true of all of us, I think, that our achievements are more often conditioned by the manner in which we behave ourselves than by the foolish daydreams and illusions we so often accept as our goals in life. This is why manners are of such overriding importance everywhere both in personal life and in the affairs of nations. The

individual cannot do anything about the beast in himself; but he can help a lot, and make life more tolerable for his friends and neighbors, by trying to act as though the beast did not exist. [12]

That happy Deist Ben Franklin could not have given a better formula for cheating the Devil and turning private vice into public virtue. Yet, juxtaposed with his view of modern society, Kennan's devotion to methods and manners is anomalous. During the 1950s Kennan interpreted the totalitarian challenge to the world as primarily an ideological one, which could be met only by moral example. [13] Becoming increasingly concerned about the moral and political health of Western, especially American, civilization, Kennan's principal criticism was directed precisely at a materialistic, mechanistic society that had lost sight of its purpose in a preoccupation with means.

Chief among the objects of Kennan's social criticism are the disintegration of community and the debasement of human labor wrought by the machine. Bicycling down a country road in Wisconsin in the summer of 1936, Kennan regretted the barrier to social intercourse erected by impersonal machines hurtling past one another. Nostalgically longing for a bygone day, he lamented the diminution of social life in the modern age:

> I thought, by way of contrast, of the sociable English highway of Chaucer's day, sometimes full of human danger but full, also, of life and companionship. It seemed to me that we had impoverished ourselves by the change; and I could not, after the years in Europe, accustom myself to it. [14]

This passage is significant for what it omits as well as for what it mentions. The reader would not discover here that at this time America was plunged into the depths of the Depression. As his reaction to Marxism suggested, Kennan's selective social judgment ignores certain material features of modern industrial capitalism.

Kennan's attraction to the remaining pre-modern spheres of Russian life grew in proportion as his disaffection for the machine deepened. Despite American stupidities and Russian hostility in the dark days of his Moscow ambassadorship, he fondly recalls pleasurable hours spent at the suburban Moscow *dacha* of Associated Press correspondent Thomas Whitney, surrounded by the life-giving, joyful work of peasants on the great Russian earth. The enchantment of the atmosphere was derived not only from the charm of the Russian summer,

> but also from the fact that it was a pre-industrial life that I was privileged here to observe: a life in which people were doing things with their hands, with animals and with Nature, a life little touched by any form of modernization, a pre-World War I and prerevolutionary life. . . . How much richer and more satisfying was human existence, after all, when there was not too much of the machine. [15]

Alarmed by the moral and social quality of American life, Kennan deplored particularly "a crass materialism and anti-intellectualism on the one hand, and . . . a marked tendency toward standardization and conformity on the other." [16] A society adept at the manipulation of means had created an unprecedented level of material abundance, along with a parallel degree of moral vacuity and personal unhappiness. From a humanistic standpoint, Kennan's response to the cultural disorder is intelligible; given an equation of methods with the "quality of life," his position makes little sense:

> First, there is the disintegration of real community life almost everywhere, as a result of the revolutionary innovations in transportation and communications that the last half century have brought us. Secondly, there is the growing domination of cultural and recreational activity by commercial media, usually connected with the advertising profession, whose motivation has little, if anything, to do with the deeper sense of human welfare. [17]

Kennan's social criticism combines astute, humane insight and glaring lacunae of understanding. When he traveled to the University of Chicago in 1951 to deliver his famous lectures, *American Diplomacy: 1900–1950*, he remarked, "I believed then deeply in the Middle West, and still do—in its essential decency, its moral earnestness, its latent emotional freshness. I viewed it, and view it now, as the heart of the moral strength of the United States. This was precisely why I was so sensitive to its imperfections." [18] He found the Hyde Park area around the University dirty, decrepit, and rude. Old men sat on street corners, vacantly staring into the distance; younger men actually went hatless and tieless, neglecting to latch their shoes and even wearing blue overcoats; teenagers were sloppily clad, and they rough-housed in a displeasing manner. Like many members of his class, George Kennan neither understands nor likes working-class and poor people, and this blind spot impairs his comprehension of, and ability to deal with, a democratic society. His thinly veiled repugnance for lower-class people makes explicable his inclination in 1936 to think of Chaucerian English highways instead of the exploitation and poverty around him.

Later in 1951 Kennan journeyed to California, where he felt that he beheld the future of America. What he saw filled him with apprehension, an apprehension that we, a quarter of a century afterwards, can appreciate. Kennan harbored grave misgivings about these people's "mortal dependence on two liquids—oil and water," the consumption of oil due largely to their "utter dependence on the costly uneconomical gadget called the automobile for practically every process of life (ibid., p. 81)." In California, where the car had effected a "clean sweep of all the patterns of living (ibid.)," the revolutionary impact of the machine age was more pronounced than elsewhere in the country. California was the end of America's quest for a new life, and here one might trace the lineaments of the future. If the national character were being forged anew in California, circumstances here and their implications merited special interest. Endowed with even richer resources and more luxuriant conditions than much of America, California life had created a hedonistic, infantile character type. When exceptional circumstances free a man from historic social restraints and material deprivation, Kennan reflected,

> the effect is to render him childlike in many respects: fun-loving, quick to laughter and enthusiasm, unanalytical, unintellectual, outwardly expansive, preoccupied with physical beauty and prowess, given to sudden and unthinking seizures of aggressiveness, driven constantly to protect his status in the group by an eager conformism—yet not unhappy. In this sense, Southern California, together with all that tendency of American life which it typifies, is childhood without the promise of maturity—with the promise only of a continual widening and growing impressiveness of the childhood world. (P. 82)

The political result of the social and moral character being formed in California threatened to be fatal to the liberal-democratic tradition as America has known it. When affluence and permissiveness will finally have reached their inevitable end, "it will be—as everywhere among children—the cruelest and most ruthless natures who will seek to protect their interests by enslaving the others; and the others, being only children, will be easily enslaved (ibid.)." Kennan expected that the hard-won values and institutions of Western civilization would perish, that "a 'latinization' of political life" might occur; if democracy survived at all, it would likely be "a romantic-Garibaldian type of democracy (p. 83)," based upon the domination of pliant, insensate masses by a man on horseback. Latin America had tempered this kind of political system with "a great ecclesiastical and civil tradition," insuring the preservation of a dignified civilization. In contrast, if such a political order were to emerge from the corruption of our national character, it would "subvert our basic political tradition (ibid.)" and expose America's urban, industrial society to an insidious despotism. Kennan may be wrong about the "latinization" of American politics, but his assessment of the fate of American democracy is not entirely dissimilar to what Tocqueville imagined as the triumph of a soft despotism in democratic society. This fate would be paradoxical, for while American abundance and expansiveness have been prime ingredients in the success of democracy, their very presence has tended to thwart our political maturation. "American abundance has fulfilled the promise of democracy; yet by virtue of this fact it has allowed Americans to become escapists seeking an "easier life" and thus never to face the problem of "man as a member of a crowded and inescapable political community"[11] (ibid.)."

America to Kennan's mind does not stand alone at the threshold of a dark age. In the *Memoirs* he relates the mixed reactions of "a love-hate complex" toward England that he felt during the year of 1957–1958, when he delivered his Reith Lectures. He disliked intensely the aspects of modernity in Oxford such as the shabby, "sexless," "inhuman" motorcyclists racing up High Street; the overcrowded, standardized stores attended by their "bored, indifferent shopgirls"; the congested, polluted streets; the "bleakness" of English parks and avenues; the absence of servants for his temporary home. Even the pre-modern "maddening casualness and impracticality in material matters" of the British disturbed him (p. 263). Notwithstanding these disagreeable realities, there was noble Merton College across from his quarters and the majestic Codrington Library at All Souls, giving him the sense that

all about me in the colleges, values were being cultivated, traditions pursued, and ancient customs—sound, symbolic, significant customs—perpetuated, in all of which I—a conservative person, a natural-born antiquarian, a firm believer in the need for continuity across the generations in form and ceremony—could only take comfort and delight. (P. 264)

Not least, Kennan was grateful for the kind and gracious hospitality of an "exquisitely civilized people." "A gloomy Scot" at heart, all the same, Kennan felt a sense of uneasiness, even inferiority, in the Oxford atmosphere, and he rebelled "as an Anglo-American and almost as a Britisher himself" against a part of Britain to which he never really belonged (ibid.).

Above all, Kennan was deeply distressed at how England appeared to be following in America's path. He was appalled by the overpopulation of the island and resentful of the manner in which the lower middle class had displaced the old upper class since the war. Sickened by "the headlong Americanization of so much of the country's life (p. 265)," he blamed the British themselves for wanting to imitate America and concluded that America stood in relation to Britain as California did to America. He disapproved British entry into the Common Market and believed Britain should avoid further industrialization, reduce her population, and cultivate economic autarchy.

> Perhaps it was a mere nostalgia for things irreparably past; perhaps it was that I loved what I saw of the older England more than many Englishmen appeared to do; the fact remains that I could develop little enthusiasm for the prospect of Britain's advancing into the modern age. I was more concerned to speculate on the means by which she might contrive to preserve some of the precious and unique features of her own past. (P. 266)

The idea broached in some circles of connecting England with the Continent by a tunnel under the Channel struck Kennan as "some sort of death urge (ibid.)."

Kennan's conservative humanism is illustrated by another issue, one closer to his own life: the training of the diplomatic profession. Years ago Kennan had criticized the incipient specialization in both the teaching and the conduct of international affairs. It was folly, he reasoned, to approach foreign policy without a basic understanding of human life and relations imparted by the liberal arts. This preparation included the formation of sensibility and character as well as intellectual discipline. Hence, the most suitable training for the Foreign Service continued to be a humanistic education. [19] The development of his profession proved not to be to Kennan's liking. He did not favor the reforms proposed for the Foreign Service by a committee under Dr. Henry Wriston of Brown University. The enlargement of the diplomatic corps, the emphasis on specialized skills rather than the cultivation of the officer, and the general lowering of standards troubled Kennan. For if "the Foreign Service be regarded as a *way of life*, rather than merely a job, then there is indeed a sense in which it is vitally important that every officer be a 'generalist'—and that is in his quality as a person of character, intellect and good judgment." [20] Kennan was dejected by a trend within the Foreign Service that seemed "in tune with an age committed to bigness, to over-organization, to depersonalization, to the collective rather than individual relationship." [21]

It must have been with a heavy heart that Kennan experienced the changes that had overtaken his profession by the time he assumed his last post, the ambassadorship to Yugoslavia from 1961 to 1963. His *Memoirs* speak touchingly of his respect and affection for the members of his staff, "men of a different generation than my own," who rose in "a different sort of bureaucratic environment: less human, less personal, vaster, more inscrutable, less reassuring." The new type of officer possessed a "studied absence of color," often serving as "a protective camouflage," and tended "to be wary, correct, faithfully pedantic, but withdrawn and in a sense masked." [22] As "the relic of an age when diplomacy was considered an art rather than a skill," a member of a vanishing breed of diplomatists for whom "style was of the essence," [23] Kennan did what he could to give the work of these men greater interest and meaning.

Kennan's humanism ill agrees with his realist emphasis on the primacy of means and methods. This difficulty is compounded when he attempts to apply Christian principles to politics. Part of the problem in this issue arises from the fact that Kennan, like most Protestants, does not accept the natural-law philosophy of morality. If one rejects the position that a knowable structure of reality exists and that a determinate nature provides the measure of human actions, then it is futile to talk philosophically about the fittingness of ends in personal or collective behavior. Even if one does not admit the rational nature of morality, however, it is unlikely that many Protestant thinkers would, as does Kennan, dismiss all consideration of the end of man. Christian morality, according to Kennan, pertains to the methods rather than purpose of political life because we can never anticipate what the results of our actions will be. It is unclear whether he means we cannot know what the ends of politics are, or that we cannot positively predict the full ramifications of an action. These, of course, are not identical points, and our limited knowledge never allows the latter. Kennan seems to say political ends are unknowable; with method, on the contrary, "one can hardly go wrong." [24] Thus:

A government can pursue its purpose in a patient and conciliatory and understanding way, respecting the interests of others and infusing its behavior with a high standard of decency and honesty and humanity, or it can show itself petty, exacting, devious, and self-righteous. If it behaves badly, even the most worthy of purposes will be apt to be polluted; whereas sheer good manners will bring some measure of redemption to even the most disastrous undertaking. The Christian citizen will be on sound ground, therefore, in

looking sharply to the methods of his government's diplomacy, even
when he is uncertain about its purposes. (Ibid.)

This passage presents the sort of ambiguity that frequently
punctuates Kennan's writing. Most probably he does not mean
"sheer good manners" and "a patient and conciliatory and
understanding way" will justify any political or diplomatic
action. If he merely means that these qualities are morally
preferable to their opposites, that does not preclude judgment
about policy aims, assuming ends are knowable. Why, anyway,
are these qualities morally superior to others, unless they are
derived from a conception of who man is and what he is for?
Further, a failed purpose, or "disastrous undertaking," is not
the same as an unknown or unintelligible purpose. Immediately
after taking this position with regard to political methods,
Kennan submitted a moral judgment about the use of nuclear
weapons. While conceding the necessity and inevitability of
force in international relations, Kennan was convinced that the
employment of nuclear weapons "goes further than anything
the Christian ethic can properly accept (ibid., p. 47)." I happen
to share his view of nuclear weapons, but my conclusion about
the instruments of war rests upon prior judgments about the
end of political life and the criteria for a just war.

In the same essay where he posits the primacy of means in
Christian ethics, Kennan makes substantive moral judgments
on the purpose of society. As he began to take a different view
of the cold war from that of "Mr. X," he reevaluated the
Russian and American societies. Kennan perceived Russia to be
evolving toward a traditional authoritarian state, to which he
was sympathetically disposed. Serious criticisms of American
society arose in his mind. For, as he saw the matter, "if you
consider, as I do, that the value of a democratic society in the
Christian sense depends not just on the fact of its enjoying
certain rights and liberties but on the nature of the use made of

them, then I think you have to raise questions about our American society of this day (p. 45)." This statement certainly implies that a judgment on the purpose of political life is both possible and incumbent upon men. Kennan's passing reference to the value of democracy "in the Christian sense" does not help to clarify his intention. Kennan has a vision of the nature and purpose of society, although it stands at variance with a pragmatic devotion to methods. America was moving ever more rapidly away from a traditional society; yet Kennan entertained the hope that Russia, having shed her totalitarian character, held promise for the future:

> While the full-blown totalitarian state in all its unnatural, nightmarish horror is certainly an abomination in the sight of God, one cannot say this of the conservative authoritarian state which has been the norm of Western society in the Christian era. And we must not forget that it is in this direction that the Soviet government, as distinct from the Chinese Communist government, has been rapidly evolving since Stalin's death. (Ibid.)

A century and a half ago Alexis de Tocqueville speculated that Russia and the United States, starting at different points, would gradually converge in a common condition. Kennan appears in recent years to have adopted a comparable view. An essay of his advances the belief "that the totalitarian phenomenon is a temporary malady which strikes societies and which bears within it the seeds of its own destruction—not a sort of permanent enslavement which can be imposed upon mankind." [25] Some kind of conservative authoritarian state "has been throughout the ages the normal lot of mankind," [26] and our liberal Anglo-American form of government is really the chance convergence of people, geography, circumstance, and time. At the present stage of history the bureaucratic, technological societies of Russia and the West are marching inexorably in the same direction:

In the main, the goals and trends of Russian communism lie along the same path as those of Western liberal-industrialism. What divides the two worlds is not a difference in aim—what divides them is fear, timidity, the unsolved problem of eastern Europe, and the unhappy dynamics of a weapons race so absorbing that both sides tend to forget the issues of its origin. [27]

Kennan deplored the self-destructive tendency of modern industrial society. The West's indifference toward the effects of overpopulation, its plunder of the natural environment, and especially "the cult of production-for-production's sake . . . the fetish of economic growth as an absolute good, which pervades the thinking of our time,"[28] portended dire consequences. Granted that the material necessities of all willing to work must be satisfied, the process of infinite growth offered the prospect only of social chaos and environmental ruin. Western society had more of a need for "an ideology which showed man how to live successfully in a quantitatively stable context, but with real possibilities for qualitative progress, than for one which abandons itself to a process of endless expansions, the ultimate results of which are beyond calculation and control, but almost certainly undesirable."[29] Again calling attention to the deterioration of the social fabric and the natural environment, Kennan registered strong doubt whether a solution would be possible within our liberal-democratic, free-enterprise tradition.[30] He posed no alternative, insisting simply there must be some middle course between our obsolete individualism and the despotic method of the Soviets. If what he said earlier, however, about the similarity between Russia and the West is true, the problem runs more deeply than the differences between state socialism and welfare capitalism.

The Western lust for technological innovation and for more speed and convenience quickened concomitantly with modern man's inability to find personal satisfaction in his life and work.

Technology, asserted Kennan, must be subjected to strict social control: "Let science, by all means, be free. But its application to human life must be the object of man's sharpest mistrust, and of the most severe social discipline."[31] Western society can no longer afford to drift along without definite objectives and careful scrutiny of the effects of its actions. Rethinking the place of political policy and the ends toward which society was moving, Kennan believed that government should assume an active role in molding the quality of life. Actually, this was only a matter of consciously doing what it already permitted, or failed to permit, by inadvertence: "The question is whether the state is to acknowledge responsibility for that shaping of the individual life which is already occurring by the processes which it tolerates or directs."[32] Kennan once indicated what he would regard as achieving "spiritual distinction" in our national life: eliminating racism, physically and politically cleaning up our cities, eradicating juvenile delinquency, restoring a sense of citizenship to urban inhabitants, instituting a proper educative role for the mass media, and protecting the environment.[33] Most readers will agree these represent eminently worthy goals; whether "spiritual distinction" would result from these achievements raises another question. What precise role government might play in improving the quality of life is also uncertain, for it was clear to him that government could neither tell men what their interests were nor, indeed, construct the "good life" for them.[34] Thus, while calling for the solution of massive social and political problems, Kennan denies that government can tell people what to do. Yet his proposal that government develop public transportation, banish commercial advertising from the public media, and preserve the natural environment obviously means government will make a judgment about the true interests of some people and, accordingly, tell others what to do. One responsibility of government, Kennan intimated, is to insure the continued existence of a privileged class that could act as a model of superior taste and accomplishment:

> I would like to stress that the objective is not to prohibit by force the vulgarity and triviality of leisure and amusements, but to offer another possibility. It is a matter of preserving a minority, or, if you prefer, an elite . . . a minority with different tastes which can in a way serve as an example of the good life.[35]

Kennan's criticism of others for failing to grapple with our domestic problems is valid, though somewhat unfair, given his own ambiguity and ambivalence. Resigned that neither liberals nor conservatives in America have even correctly perceived these problems, Kennan records "a growing intellectual loneliness on my part and a feeling of inability to contribute usefully to current discussion."[36] Since attention to foreign affairs seemed futile in face of America's internal dilemmas, Kennan found himself a rueful spectator of historical decline.

George Kennan possesses a vision, but this vision and his character are incompatible with the concept of realism as he presents it. In his vision of life an Arnoldian humanism mingles with a residual Calvinism, and neither this vision nor his highly subjective temperament is harmonious with his purported pragmatic objectivity. Kennan's professed realism is in fact diametrically opposed to his humanistic philosophy of man and society. It was no realist who, visiting bombed-out Hamburg after the war, recalled a higher moral law at the heart of civilized existence:

> If the Western world was really going to make valid the pretense of a higher moral departure point—of greater sympathy and understanding for the human being as God made him, as expressed not only in himself but in the things he had wrought and cared about—then it had to learn to fight its wars morally as well as militarily, or not fight them at all; for moral principles were a part of its strength. Shorn of this strength, it was no longer itself; its

victories were not real victories; and the best it would accomplish in the long run would be to pull down the temple over its own head. [37]

Kennan's tragic view of history leaves him an outsider to the Faustian spirit of his age. There is no place in the modern enterprise of nature's conquest for his belief in the fallen, finite nature of man. Nonetheless, Kennan's mind seems divided, leaving him bound to a legacy he knows to be spent. This ambivalence is exemplified by his attitude toward the Anglo-Saxon political heritage and the broader cultural matrix in which it has developed. The reader will remember Kennan's fear of the possible "political latinization" of North America as well as his apparent inability to transcend the liberal-democratic tradition to solve the problems generated by it. At the end of his first volume of *Memoirs* Kennan tells us of a report on Latin America he once submitted to the State Department that was filed away in obscurity because of its sharply provocative nature. Pointing out the tragic element in Latin experience, Kennan nevertheless pays eloquent praise to a character very different from his own and his society's:

The human existence is everywhere tragic; that of Latin America is only tragic in its own manner; and this is a manner in some respects less menacing, certainly less apocalyptic, than that in which tragedy threatens to manifest itself elsewhere. Everywhere else, too, the human ego—demonic, anarchic, unbridleable—interferes in men's affairs and claims its own in their behavior. I am not sure that I do not prefer it in its Latin American manifestations: spontaneous, uninhibited, and full-throated, rather than in those carefully masked and poisonously perverted forms it assumes among the Europeans and the Anglo-Americans. Latin America is the only one of the world's great subdivisions where the human being is still entirely human, where no one has nuclear weapons or is even thinking of developing them, where the great fund of precept and experience and custom that has been created in the Christian West to reconcile man with God and with the requirements of a civilized condition is still wholly relevant. The South American continent may prove some day to be the last repository and custodian of humane Christian values that men in the European motherlands and in North America—overfed, overorganized, and blinded by fear and ambition—have thrown away. [38]

This portrait of the South and North American character expresses an ambivalence within its author. George Kennan's attraction to the genuine human values of Latin civilization reveals a portion of his spirit out of joint not only with his times, but with the heart of "a gloomy Scot" and with the mind of a realist.

2

Realism and Foreign Policy

ACCORDING TO GEORGE KENNAN'S DOCTRINE OF REALISM, AN inherent conflict exists between the pressures of democratic politics and the effective conduct of foreign affairs. To Kennan's mind professional diplomacy ought to serve the national purpose rather than particular interests, and he sees the period 1945–1949 as one of those rare times when "America's peacetime diplomacy may be said to have had its own integrity as purely an exercise in foreign policy." [1] This situation began to change after the election in 1948 of President Truman, who allowed partisan politics to intrude again upon diplomacy. The "pure" function of career diplomacy is "a matter of duty, dedication, reason and integrity"; domestic politics, Kennan feels, on the other hand, is a "sordid, never-ending Donnybrook among pampered and inflated egos," unavoidable in a democracy but productive of little good. [2] Whatever the foibles of democratic diplomacy, Kennan does not doubt the essential decency and benignity of America's intention in her postwar foreign relations; yet he remains

48

convinced that "had my views on Russia been heeded during the wartime period, a number of our problems and embarrassments of the postwar period might have been alleviated." [3]

Having served as diplomatic secretary at the American embassy in Moscow from 1933 to 1937, Kennan returned to Moscow in 1944 as minister-counselor to Ambassador Averell Harriman. While under Harriman, Kennan drew up a report, apparently ignored at the time, in which he staked out some of the premises of his later "X" article. In "Russia—Seven Years Later" Kennan argued that Soviet expansion was following the traditional path of czarist diplomacy and that Russia's postwar policy would aim at the completion of what she had begun in 1939. Russia, he explained, was not nearly so interested in spreading Communism as in establishing power and dominion in central and eastern Europe; ideology took second place to the practical end of power politics. He predicted that Western men of good will would not understand Russia because of the Kremlin's secrecy and suspicion—its "Chinese wall of the spirit"—and that the West could never begin to fathom the Russian mind until it learned to appreciate Russia's ability to deal in contradictions and her refusal to recognize objective criteria of right and wrong, reality and unreality. [4]

At the end of the war Kennan set down his ideas concerning the satellite areas and adumbrated some conclusions of the "X" article in a report entitled "Russia's International Position at the Close of the War with Germany." The greatest transformation wrought by the war lay not in the development of Russia herself, but in the collapse of the countries around her. Soviet policy-makers faced the task of consolidating their new responsibilities and making them a source of strength rather than weakness, as they had been for the czars. In their effort the Soviets would encounter problems of administration, agricultural production, and personnel, together with all the vicissitudes of an extended, diverse empire. Marxism as a revolutionary ideology had lost its spiritual hold on the Russian people; the Soviet government, therefore, was counting on the naive American hope that collaboration would be possible if only cordial relations were established. Instead, then, of being duped into recognizing her puppet governments and giving Russia aid, the West should stand firm. If this happened, Russia would do her best to create tension in the West, but this would be her last card, and in time she would have to withdraw (ibid., pp. 532–46).

Kennan's political reports were buried in obscurity, and he remained an unheeded prophet. Immediately after the war he advocated acceptance of a division of Europe into spheres of interest. Conditions rendered both joint control and disengagement impossible, he maintained, so dismemberment was necessary to resist totalitarianism. Although the United States could do nothing about the de facto Russian hegemony in East Europe, Kennan felt that we should not share responsibility for Russia's actions by giving her aid of any kind. He opposed economic aid to Russia because it would serve her interests while impairing our own. Financial aid was unfeasible because people and regime "were bound together in a common dialectical relationship" such that we could not help or hurt one without doing the same to the other (p. 275). The wisest policy for America was to do nothing, and anyway, he added, Russia's hardships were her problem.

Kennan's official anonymity came to an end with his telegraphic message from Moscow on February 22, 1946. He had received an irate note from Washington asking him to account for recent Soviet behavior in refusing to join the World Bank and International Monetary Fund. His Long Telegram further delineated the terms upon which the doctrine of containment was later based. Marxist theses about Communism and capitalism, he asserted, were utterly "baseless and disproven" and were merely the ideological façade for a deep neurosis. Internal necessities drove the Kremlin to what was admittedly only traditional Russian nationalism, but Marxist ideological trappings severely exacerbated this aggressiveness. The Kremlin's secrecy, conspiratorial fantasies, and imperviousness to objective truth made normal diplomatic relations impossible. Kennan anticipated Soviet actions and suggested what the American response ought to be. At this point an ambiguity entered his explanation of the conflict. The Soviet Union was a fanatical political power dedicated to the destruction of American society and America's international position; nevertheless, the threat could be met without recourse to war. Kennan followed this assurance with the observation that, since Soviet strategy was neither schematic nor adventuristic, the Russians would retreat if confronted with force. Soviet power, he wrote, is

> impervious to logic of reason, and it is highly sensitive to logic of force. For this reason it can easily withdraw—and usually does— when strong resistance is encountered at any point. Thus, if the adversary has sufficient force and makes clear his readiness to use it, he rarely has to do so. (Pp. 557–58)

Reading this report, Kennan's superiors in Washington would reasonably have taken his view of Soviet responsiveness to the "logic of force" as calling for military containment. This is, at least, the plausible interpretation of his words. In 1946 Kennan was called home to be deputy of foreign affairs at the newly established National War College. Speaking before State Department personnel in September of that year, he said that Soviet behavior could be altered only "by the logic of a long-term set of circumstances which makes it evident that noncollaborative purposes on their part will not pay—will redound to Russia's disadvantage, whereas a more kindly policy toward us would win them advantages (p. 303)." The precise nature of these conditioning factors was unclear. On a speaking tour in the Midwest and West in the summer of 1946, Kennan deplored the mounting, hysterical anti-Communism, but, while conceding a degree of merit in Marxist theory, he reaffirmed that Russia must be forcefully held in check. The United States still had world opinion on her side, and that edge "should enable us, if our policies are wise and nonprovocative to contain them both militarily and politically for a long time to come (p. 304)."

In the early spring of 1947 Kennan worked on a special committee that studied the question of aid to Greece and Turkey. He subsequently disavowed the policy that emerged and became known as the Truman Doctrine. Kennan states that he recommended only political and economic aid to Greece, but the Pentagon intervened and persuaded Truman to give military assistance to both countries. Kennan opposed the Truman Doctrine because of its militaristic approach and "because of the sweeping nature of the commitments which it implied (pp. 319–20)."

Later that spring Secretary of State George Marshall selected Kennan to establish the Policy Planning Staff in the State Department, a group responsible for conducting strategic studies and formulating long-term policy. The Marshall Plan for the economic reconstruction of Europe, announced in June 1947, was the product of the Staff and especially of Kennan himself. The Marshall Plan was more in line with his view of foreign policy. It "finally broke through the confusion of wartime pro-Sovietism, wishful thinking, anglophobia and self-righteous punitivism in which our occupational policies in Germany had thus far been enveloped, and placed us at long last on what was, and for six years remained, a constructive and sensible path (p. 335)." Unlike the Truman Doctrine, he explained, the Marshall Plan was not merely a defensive reaction to Communist pressure, nor was it a blank check for aid. Europeans were to assume principal responsibility for their economic rehabilitation, and German recovery was considered a *sine qua non* for any viable new order. By the time he wrote the second volume of his *Memoirs,* Kennan seemed to feel that a prudent American policy had lasted less than six years. There he writes that the proper policy toward Russia obtained between 1948 and 1950; this was "the moderate Marshall Plan approach—an approach aimed at *creating* strength in the West rather than *destroying* strength in Russia." [5] The United States faced "a long-term effort of rivalry and pressure by means short of general war," [6] but after 1950 our policy disastrously devolved into the folly of liberation. Although the *Memoirs* makes clear his disapproval of the State Department's strident anti-Communism, Kennan said nothing of it in his celebrated essay, "The Sources of Soviet Conduct," published in July 1947, which by no means opposed the growing militarization of American foreign policy.

Signed anonymously as "Mr. X," Kennan's article in *Foreign Affairs* immediately provoked a storm of controversy that has scarcely abated after a generation. The basic themes of the "X" article had been outlined in his previous reports: Soviet aggression was based on the unobjective, internal necessity of justifying Stalin's dictatorial authority at home; an intractable antagonism toward the West would persist until the nature of Soviet power itself changed; and, given Soviet imperviousness to objective reality, the United States must prepare for a protracted cold war of containing Russian expansion. Kennan subsequently claimed that he was talking about the political containment of a political threat, but "Mr. X" unequivocally stated that the Soviet Union would retrench only under compulsion, "stopping only when it meets with some unanswerable force. . . . Thus the Kremlin has no compunction about retreating in the face of superior force." [7] The "X" article expressly advocated the exercise of "counter-force" against Russian expansion in a "duel of infinite duration":

In the light of the above, it will be clearly seen that the Soviet pressure against the free institutions of the Western world is something that can be contained by the adroit and vigilant application of counter-force at a series of constantly shifting geographical and political points, corresponding to the shifts and maneuvers of Soviet policy, but which cannot be charmed or talked out of existence. [8]

"Mr. X's" realism did not deter him from proclaiming America's manifest destiny in the world. He concluded on a moralistic note, thanking "Providence which, by providing the American people with this implacable challenge, has made their entire security as a nation dependent on their pulling themselves together and accepting the responsibilities of moral and political leadership that history plainly intended them to bear." [9]

Kennan has not clarified his intention in the "X" article by telling us in the *Memoirs*: "What I said in the X-Article was not intended as a doctrine. I am afraid that when I think about foreign policy, I do not think in terms of doctrines. I think in terms of principles." [10] With respect to a military or nonmilitary response to Russia, the distinction offered here is elusive. Although Kennan claimed, in the aftermath of the "X" article, that his readers had misunderstood him, he made no attempt to dispel those false impressions. On the contrary, in an article that appeared shortly before his resignation from the Policy Planning Staff in late 1949 he wrote that world stability in the current abnormal conditions rested upon American military power: "Prominent among these factors is the maintenance by this country of a powerful and impressive armed forces establishment, commensurate with the great responsibilities we are being forced to assume in the life of the world community." [11] In none of Kennan's writing does there appear the faintest reference to economic interests at stake in the cold war. But on this occasion he raised a doubt about the reliability of Britain and the Continent as markets:

Basically, they boil down to the question of how Great Britain and the crowded, industrialized countries of Western Europe are going to earn the money, even with their restored production, to buy the food and raw materials which they require from overseas areas, and particularly from North America. [12]

Kennan criticized the American response to events in Europe in late 1947 and early 1948, especially in reaction to the fall of Czechoslovakia, leading to the formation of NATO. He had foretold a Russian "baring of the fangs" if the West should stand firm, and now myopic and parochial thinking in Washington and a misinterpretation of the "X" article were producing a further militarization of policy in the form of NATO. NATO, he objected, represented "the vast, turgid, self-centered, and highly emotional process by which the views and reactions of official Washington were finally evolved." [13] On his part he lost interest "for remaining in a profession where passivity, inscrutability and tactical ingenuity were valued so highly, and serious analytical effort—so little." [14] Basic philosophical differences between Kennan and the State Department, centering chiefly on the militarization of policy and over-extension of commitments, compelled him to resign from the Policy Planning Staff in December 1949 and to leave government altogether in June 1950. In his swan song from government service, a dispatch entitled "The Soviet Union and the Atlantic Pact," which Kennan says is the best statement of his public views, he contended that Russia had no intention of a military attack on the West and that our bellicose policy— exemplified by NATO, the rearmament of Germany and Japan, and our view of the meaning of Korea—was only causing her to harden her own posture and tighten domestic control. [15] Calling for a sensible balance between the political and military dimensions of policy, he wrote, "There was an incurable conflict between the ideal military posture and the goal of winning the political war." [16] This point is well taken, but it is unclear what he meant by saying, "It was not 'containment'

that failed; it was the intended follow-up that never occurred."[17] More important, if Kennan discounted the likelihood of overt Russian aggression, this could not easily have been deduced from other things he said, and omitted to say, at the time. Three years after the "X" article Kennan announced in an address before the Institute on United States Foreign Policy in Milwaukee, Wisconsin: "I believe that the basic lines of the policy which we have pursued in these past 3 years have been pretty well prescribed for us by the limits of what was possible and that they could not have been much different than they were without putting us worse off today than we actually are."[18]

In the spring of 1950 George Kennan left the State Department to join the Institute for Advanced Study at Princeton University. Now that at long last he had been raised from professional anonymity and his ideas apparently adopted as official policy, he protested that everyone had egregiously misunderstood him. Insisting that what he always meant was the political containment of a political threat, Kennan publicly criticized the militarization of American foreign policy. Military conflict was not only inappropriate but futile, he maintained, and Russia must be allowed to work out her own fate. Hopefully, the Kremlin might lift the Iron Curtain a bit, ease domestic control, and cease its aggressive expansion.[19] During the Korean War he condemned the war hysteria in certain quarters, imploring: "As long as there is a one-thousandth chance that a major world conflict can be avoided—and I hold the chance far greater than that—let us guard that chance like the apple of our eye."[20] The spreading Red scare at home and the perversion of the national character in the battle against Communism were among the most deleterious effects of the cold war. Communism, Kennan stressed, was primarily an external danger, and the worst result possible was "that we should become like them" in the struggle. Let us not be diverted from real problems, he pleaded, "into reactions which threaten us with the loss of the national soul."[21]

These counsels of prudence notwithstanding, Kennan's writings do not provide a consistent interpretation of the cold war and its resolution. A focus upon theory or objective behavior led to quite different conclusions. If one held that Soviet international conduct was not essentially different from that of all great powers, and if one viewed her conduct as typical of traditional Russian nationalism, then the resolution of the conflict acquired a different shape from what it would if one assumed that Marxist theory dictated an implacable aggressiveness. If, moreover, one argued, as Kennan had, that American actions had contributed to the intensification of the cold war, then it would be wrong to attribute total responsibility for the cold war to an irrational Soviet ideology. Yet in his later *Memoirs*, despite previous criticism of American policy, Kennan writes that responsibility for the cold war rested "primarily in the ideological preconceptions of the Soviet leaders and particularly in the image of an ineradicable hostility between the 'bourgeois' and 'socialist' worlds which they had built up in their own minds."[22] Alternatively, Kennan has suggested that Russia's behavior was essentially that of any great nation-state. This view is consistent with his concern for the concrete effects of her objective behavior and his belief that "the most important influence that the United States can bring to bear upon internal developments in Russia will continue to be the influence of example."[23] In this vein he called upon his countrymen to substitute moral suasion for an atomic holocaust, and he hoped that the power of national example would over the long run induce modifications in the nature of Russian Communism itself.

While sometimes arguing, then, that an irrational, subjective Soviet ideology generated the cold war, Kennan acknowledged the fundamental antagonism between the great powers by affirming the "great ethical and philosophical differences which separate us from the Soviets." Nevertheless, he recommended a measured policy designed "to prove to [Stalin] that it would be the part of prudence on his part to moderate his behavior on the international plane." [24] As Kennan moved toward the formulation of the doctrine of disengagement, he asseverated that the change in Russian-American relations "has been more of a change in the American interpretation of external reality than in that reality itself." [25] The Soviets, he reasoned, were in the same business of national power as everyone else, nor were they much different; in fact, "the differences are relative." [26] In response to the Quaker pamphlet *Speak Truth to Power,* criticizing American cold war policy, he replied that "if modern totalitarianism is actually no more horrible than modern American democracy, the rationale of recent American foreign policy does indeed break down at many points. Admittedly, the differences between the one and the other are differences of degree. But are they unimportant?" [27] Considering Kennan's own shifts of emphasis regarding Soviet conduct and theory, it is understandable why some men came to think that "containment and liberation are only two sides of the same coin." [28] Kennan meant by this that both ideas were part of the larger problem of how to mold America's conduct so as to inspire her allies' confidence and her enemies' respect. This explanation possesses an air of abstraction and unreality to which Robert Tucker has tried to give historical substance. Noting the fateful ambiguity between a conventional desire for security and an erroneously inflated notion of security (a notion tied to the internal order of states as well as to a balance of power between them, and dependent on all states, not just some), Tucker concludes that through "a dialectic as old as the history of statecraft, expansion proved to be the other side of the coin of containment." [29] To contain the expansion of others we ourselves had to expand, and in this fashion the limited aim of security evolved into a desire to uphold "a stable world order that would insure the triumph of liberal-capitalist values." [30] The convertibility of a defensive policy of containment into an aggressive policy of liberation was perhaps in Kennan's mind when he remarked that the differences between Truman's and Dulles's policies were ones of "rhetoric and style" rather than substance. [31]

The thesis of disengagement appeared in Kennan's *Realities of American Foreign Policy* (1954), but the full explication of the doctrine did not come until his provocative 1957 Reith Lectures, which were broadcast by the BBC and published the following year as *Russia, the Atom, and the West*. [32] The Russian threat to the West, according to Kennan, was political, not military. Her objective was to exploit the weaknesses within our civilization and to sow disunity within the Western world. The only way of winning the cold war was to attend to our internal problems and improve the moral quality of our civilization. The challenge, in actuality, lay inside rather than beyond America's shores: "Whether we win against the Russians is primarily a question of whether we win against ourselves." [33]

In the Reith Lectures Kennan maintained that world tensions revolved around the German question because Russia would never withdraw her forces from Eastern and Central Europe until American forces were out of West Germany. The division of Germany was justified in the immediate postwar era, but that condition was no longer either feasible or desirable. He advocated the unification of Germany following the removal of all foreign troops from her soil. Germany's future military status would have to be severely restricted in order to assuage Russia's fear of a reunited Germany; even so, evacuating Soviet forces from Eastern and Central Europe was preferable to supporting a German army to oppose them. Kennan rejected atomic weapons as "a temporary and regrettable expedient" no longer suitable to an effective foreign policy, proposing that Europe assume her own defense. For this purpose paramilitary forces of an internal police nature were adequate. A foreign policy based upon atomic weapons was ultimately bankrupt: "The true end of political actions is, after all, to affect the deeper convictions of men; this the atomic bomb cannot do. . . . There can be no coherent relations between such a weapon and the normal objects of national policy." [34]

The militarization of foreign policy represented by NATO along with America's vastly overextended commitments were sharply reproved by Kennan. He urged a de-emphasis on NATO and a general contraction of America's overseas responsibilities. Both a reliance on diplomatic coalitions and a utopian legalism in American-Soviet conflicts should be replaced by "an informational war of indefinite duration, and a quiet old-fashioned diplomatic attack on certain of the individual political problems that divide us from the Soviet world." [35] But above all, Kennan was convinced, we must enhance the quality of our own national life, for the cold war was in essence one of moral example:

> Our diplomacy can never be stronger than the impression we contrive to create on others, not just by virtue of what we *do* but rather—and even more importantly—by what we *are*. . . . Russia confronts us not just with a foreign policy or a military policy but with an integrated philosophy of action internal and external. We can respond effectively in no other way. [36]

Kennan coupled an eloquent, humane analysis of the senseless horror of atomic diplomacy with a constructive strategy for America's relations with the world. The plan of disengagement, though, met with widespread hostile reaction, including ironically that of Walter Lippmann, who earlier, in criticizing "Mr. X's" policy of containment, had advanced a similar scheme. [37] The Reith Lectures, Kennan regrets, were too late, for the "Western powers were now embarked on a path for which I had no stomach." [38] Impotent to guide history, Kennan retreated, as Henry Adams had, to its study: "The pursuit of history, the common refuge of those who find themselves helpless in the face of the present, would have made—did make, in fact, at times—a better occupation." [39]

It is not my intention here to dwell on the doctrine of containment itself. That policy has been ably analyzed and criticized by a number of writers, including William Appleman Williams, Walter Lippmann, and Robert Tucker. [40] My concern lies with realism's heuristic value in Kennan's analysis of foreign affairs. Kennan, an apostle of the school of realism in foreign affairs, holds that the successful conduct of foreign relations depends on one's taking an unideological, dispassionate, amoral view of objective reality; this done, a clear and sound policy will emerge. Yet he has not defined containment consistently, nor has he offered a perspicuous assessment of responsibility for the cold war. To Kennan's later disavowal of the policy that was pursued in the name of containment, William Appleman Williams has answered in exasperation, "Either Kennan can not accurately set down on paper what he really had in his mind, or he sought, in his recent apologia, to minimize his own responsibility during the last decade." [41] Now, I believe that Kennan possesses more literary skill and personal integrity than Williams allows him. The difficulty may be due, rather, to the formalistic nature of realism itself. Because Kennan's doctrine of realism entails no specific content of its own and can accommodate even opposing positions, it has resulted in thorough ambiguity. (The purely procedural nature of realism reminds one how, as Péguy said, Kantianism has clean hands because it has no hands at all.) Kennan's own reflections on his development from containment to disengagement do not help to explain a realistic foreign policy.

Disengagement, he later wrote, would never be possible as long as policy-makers remained bound by "that overmilitarization of thought about the cold war in the face of which no peaceful solutions of world differences are even thinkable." [42] An element of trust and risk was necessary in order to secure peace. For "the ideal military posture is simply the enemy of every political détente or compromise; and whoever is not prepared to make sacrifices and to accept risks in the military field should not lay claim to any serious desire to see world problems settled by any means short of war." [43] With the advantage of hindsight, however, Kennan seemed to offer a slightly different version of history. He had left the State Department in 1950 believing NATO to be fundamentally misconceived and unsound. A decade later he implied that NATO had merely been improperly executed, that it had never been intended "to contain militarily, in permanence, a Soviet empire extending from the Elbe to the Pacific." Instead, the mutual purpose of the Marshall Plan and NATO was "to place the West in a position where it would some day be able to negotiate the liquidation of the vast misunderstanding represented in the division of the continent." [44] These statements suggest that only illusion and error, not any real conflict of interests, stood between the great powers and that American policy-makers had committed merely a tactical blunder, not a basic strategic error. Just as Kennan tended to dissolve conflict into mistaken innocence, so too he narrowed the range of strategic alternatives. He defended the cause of disengagement by identifying the policy of the 1930s and 1940s, with which he presumably associated himself, as that of coexistence, labeling the extremist policy of liberation a peculiar aberration of the 1950s:

From 1933 to the late 1940's this was, I think, the case. But during the past ten years we have witnessed the resurgence of a body of opinion which takes the other line, which rejects in effect the whole concept of peaceful coexistence and which would commit us to a policy of "we or they"—a policy which sees no issue to the present contest except in the final and complete destruction of one side or the other. [45]

Although liberation did represent a marked shift in policy from containment, one can hardly equate containment with coexistence. To do so ignores the equivocality of containment and what Walter Lippmann called its "strategic monstrosity." Furthermore, to identify the policy of the late 1940s with that of the 1930s runs counter to Kennan's own long-standing denunciations of Roosevelt's deluded, amateurish diplomacy.

Looking back on the early years of the cold war, Kennan later implied that America's foreign policy in the postwar period had been basically correct in conception and implementation. Far from being overmilitarized, American policy was the "natural and predictable" reaction to Russian behavior. America never really opposed socialism as such. Russian power disturbed the international equilibrium, but Kennan did not definitely say that the Soviet Union had ever in fact posed a military threat to Western security:

> The cold war, let it be said most emphatically, does not exist because people in the West object to the Russian people having socialism or any other system they wish. . . . But the Soviet Union is not only an ideological phenomenon. It is also a great power, physically and militarily. Even if the prevailing ideology in Russia were not antagonistic to the concepts prevailing elsewhere, the behavior of the government of that country in its international relations, and particularly any considerable expansion of its power at the expense of the freedom of other peoples, would still be a matter of most serious interest to the world at large. [46]

The advance of Russian political and military power into eastern and central Europe in 1945 and the forceful maintenance of that power there naturally aroused the fear in the

West that Russia would subjugate other peoples. Kennan admitted that he had decried the militarization of foreign policy and the arms race in the West, but he asserted that this was the natural reaction of the West to Russian actions from World War II through Korea. He denied that economics influenced in any way the formulation of American policy. It would be foolish to regard Western policies as inspired by financiers and manufacturers, for these policies were "in large measure the natural and predictable reactions of great peoples to a situation which Moscow itself did much to create."[47]

This position is difficult to reconcile with Kennan's statements at the Graduate Institute of International Studies in Geneva in 1965. Kennan stated positively, as he had on other occasions, that at no time in the postwar period was the Russian threat ever a military one: "It was perfectly clear to anyone with even a rudimentary knowledge of the Russia of that day that the Soviet leaders had no intention of attempting to advance their cause by launching military attacks with their own armed forces across frontiers."[48] Such an undertaking suited neither Marxist theory nor Russia's urgent need for recovery after the war. Nevertheless, he added, atomic weapons could not have been abolished in 1947, despite the fact that "there was good reason to believe that the Soviet leaders did not welcome the insertion of such weapons into the military-political equation." Atomic weapons did not fit into Marxist ideology, and Stalin "seems to have been better aware than many in the West have ever been" of their limitations.[49] Kennan's realism did not always lead him to the same conclusion. In a dispatch to the Secretary of State in 1945 Kennan insisted that the Soviets would not balk at using atomic power in the most ruthless manner:

There is nothing—I repeat nothing—in the history of the Soviet regime which could justify us in assuming that the men who are now in power in Russia, or even those who have chances of assuming power within the foreseeable future, would hesitate for a moment to apply this power against us if by doing so they thought that they might materially improve their own power position in the world. . . . To assume that the Soviet leaders would be restrained by scruples of gratitude or humanitarianism would be to fly in the face of overwhelming contrary evidence on a matter vital to the future of our country. [50]

When Kennan initially unfolded the doctrine of disengagement, he wrote that the change in American-Russian relations "has been more a change in the American interpretation of external reality than in that reality itself." [51] Yet, in a fifty-year retrospective analysis of the Russian Revolution and its consequences, he reaffirmed that the cold war had been due primarily to Russia's irrational view of the West, an ideological monomania for which there was no objective basis in reality. Even though the West had been hostile to Russia, "the relationship could scarcely have been a normal one in the light of the fundamental postulates of the Bolshevik political outlook." [52]

From containment to disengagement and back again, Kennan provides neither a coherent explanation of international relations nor a consistent foreign policy. A man may, of course, change his mind over time, but the concept of realism fails to illuminate the analysis, formulation, and development of foreign policy. As Kennan employs the concept, realism does not specify any particular policy, and realism's abstraction obscures political reality by attributing conflict to misunderstanding or psychological debility rather than to real disparity of interest. Kennan's ambiguous interpretation of containment and the cold war generally derives from his preoccupation with Soviet theory and from an indeterminate conception of American interests. Like formalistic theories, realism prescinds from empirical factors; this is disconcerting in the case of realism only because of its professed attachment to objective reality. Although realism offers little clue either to Kennan's thinking or to a theory of foreign policy, perhaps we can better understand the doctrine by examining Kennan's treatment of the relation between interest, power, and morality. In his capacity as diplomatic historian and political thinker, Kennan has been concerned especially with the effective securement of national self-interest.

The gravest defect in the conduct of American foreign relations has been what Kennan calls "the legalistic-moralistic approach to international problems." This theme, he writes,

> runs like a red skein through our foreign policy of the last fifty years. . . . It is the belief that it should be possible to suppress the chaotic and dangerous aspirations of governments in the international field by the acceptance of some system of legal rules and restraints. . . . It is the essence of this belief that, instead of taking the awkward conflicts of national interest and dealing with them on their merits with a view to finding the solutions least unsettling to the stability of international life, it would be better to find some formal criteria of a judicial nature by which the permissible behavior of states could be defined. [53]

This dogma, argues Kennan, mistakenly presupposes that all states are satisfied with their present status and limits their possibilities for redress; it confers a false value upon national sovereignty, ignoring national divisions and inhibiting change; it overlooks subtler forms of aggression such as propaganda and subversion; it assumes that domestic issues cannot become international concerns; and, worst of all, it abets a moralism—"the assumption that state behavior is a fit subject for moral judgment" [54]—which gives rise to the mentality of total war and total victory.

Kennan's criticism presents a false antithesis. One can very well share his disapprobation of an over-reliance upon an excessively formalized juridical code, especially of any undue expectations regarding arbitration and enforcement, and still not be prepared to abandon all standards of judging the actions of states. Furthermore, the sort of fatuous moralism he disapproves demonstrates merely an error in practical judgment and a lack of prudence on the part of men; no serious man would equate the empty posturing of statesmen in a democratic age with the deliberate exercise of moral judgment. If we repudiate all standards of moral judgment, what then can it mean to assess the "merits" of various competing interests? Again, to seek the solution "least unsettling to the stability of international life" would be in effect to judge in favor of the preponderant power in disputes, for stability as such rests largely upon the distribution of power. Finally, experience suggests that "moralism," a totalistic mentality, and practical ruthlessness are not mutually exclusive. Kennan himself deplored the "schizophrenia" of American postwar thought, a condition created by Russia's shattering of a nineteenth-century legalistic tradition in Western diplomacy. The result, which appalled him, was American statesmen's sudden absorption with the uses of power. [55] Why should a realist condemn the callous or unscrupulous use of power, unless there are criteria of another order by which he measures the conduct of foreign relations? The statesmen whom Kennan censured were realists in a sense; yet, if state behavior transcends moral judgment, then any action, even the realism of atomic blackmail, is permissible. That Kennan never took such a position testifies to his moral sense rather than his realism.

The condition of perpetual conflict between nations, Kennan believes, stems from the Fall. Man is radically and permanently sinful; hence force and violence are necessary in life in order to constrain his sinful nature. To the Quakers who presented a case for pacifism, Kennan pointed out the consequences of man's postlapsarian fate:

> We run around, each of us, encumbered with a side of our natures—the demonic side—which is not at all pleasant, wholly

unamenable to reason, capable of great destructiveness, and extremely persistent. It manifests itself in us individually and collectively. Ultimately, it can be restrained only by some form of force. Violence is the tribute we pay to original sin. Everyone pays it, one way or another. [56]

Kennan opined that, given man's corrupted nature,

it is idle to suppose that just because we human beings have our redeeming qualities and our moments of transcendent greatness, we are "nice people." We are not. There are many times and situations when we require restraint. The problem, therefore, is not *whether* force is to be exerted but how; and this applies in the individual, the family, the nation, and the world community. [57]

Kennan's Calvinist ancestors were acutely aware of the enduring element of self-love in human nature, but they always supposed that this proclivity must be circumscribed and regulated for the common good. They would never have elevated self-interest to the norm of human conduct. Kennan sometimes calls himself a man of the eighteenth century, an apt description. Despite residual traces of his Calvinist inheritance, Kennan belongs more to the genteel world of eighteenth-century rationalism than to an earlier age that recognized, yet governed man's concupiscence. His idea of human nature accepts the comfortable rationalist identification of self-interest with the common interest. Kennan's realist critique of American foreign policy concludes with a quintessentially liberal-bourgeois faith in the natural harmony of interests. Realism means that we can know only our own interest, but a well-mannered pursuit of that interest will serve the general interest of mankind:

It will mean that we will have the modesty to admit that our own national interest is all that we are really capable of knowing and understanding—and the courage to recognize that if our purposes

and undertakings here at home are decent ones, unsullied by
arrogance or hostility toward other people or delusions of supe-
riority, then the pursuit of our national interest can never fail to be
conducive to a better world. . . . Whatever is realistic in concept,
and founded in an endeavor to see both ourselves and others as we
really are, cannot be illiberal. [58]

Kennan's Calvinist forebears did not entertain the fancy that
the common good derived automatically from the pursuit of
private goods. The transformation of private vices into public
benefits was an invention of a later, secular era.

Kennan advances his argument for the realistic pursuit of
national self-interest in *Realities of American Foreign Policy.*
While never defining the national interest, Kennan says that the
conditions of the modern world should prepare us to expect
instability and violence. The art of international politics
consists in channeling change without destroying the peace of
the world. In what direction change should be channeled, or
why peace ought to be preserved when it is not in the interest of
a particular government, Kennan leaves unanswered. At any
rate, this goal can only be accomplished through the caprices of
political expediency, not by means of moral norms or legal
structures, for objective standards of right and wrong do not
exist in international relations:

> This task will be best approached not through the establishment
> of rigid legal norms but rather by the traditional devices of political
> expediency. . . . Let us face it: in most international differences
> elements of right or wrong, comparable to those that prevail in
> personal relationships, are—if they exist at all, which is a question-
> —simply not discernible to the outsider. [59]

Do norms of right and wrong pertain to any international
disputes or state actions and, if so, to which ones and whence do
they arise? Most men will agree that excessive rigidity is
imprudent, and obviously mixed elements of right and wrong

complicate most disputes between states. Sensible men will readily concede that the conduct and responsibility of states are not identical to the conduct and responsibility of individuals. If, however, Kennan intends to say that governments are subject to no objective moral principles, he must be willing to accept the implications of this positivist position. It means, for instance, that if a certain policy works, if a government can commit an action with impunity, that action is permissible. If no rational criteria of right and wrong obtain in international affairs, there is no obligation to preserve peace.

Although we cannot transfer personal moral values to relations between states, Kennan says we ought, nevertheless, always to act in accord with our own moral values. Even so, we cannot view these values as obligatory upon others. This position differs from his unqualified assertion that only the methods, not the ends, of states are morally mensurable: "In particular, let us not assume that the *purposes* of states, as distinct from the methods, are fit subjects for measurement in moral terms." [60] Kennan seems to equate manners and morals, thereby reducing conduct to a matter of taste; yet he neglects to explain how methods or manners are morally evaluated. Also, if we ought always to act according to our own values, then Kennan, by reasoning thus, has not actually circumvented the danger of moralistic crusading, while simultaneously he has removed all restraints from state action, except the test of expediency. To forsake moralistic crusading does not require us to surrender all moral responsibility for political practice. Such a position is untenable for one who posits anything, as Kennan does, about the moral nature of man.

Elsewhere he has given a more limited version of what he means by realism in diplomacy. [61] Describing the diplomatic imbroglio that led to his resignation in 1963 as Ambassador to Yugoslavia, Kennan explains that in international relations governments influence one another by a subtle use of measures favorable and adverse to each other's interests. These "favors and injuries" need to be deployed flexibly according to circumstances in order to influence a government's policies. Ideological preconception and rigidity of the kind that motivated Congress in its interference with Yugoslavian relations upset the delicate art of diplomacy. If all Kennan meant by realism amounted to this, he could more properly speak of political prudence. This, however, does not appear to be what he commonly means by the concept of realism. Since this question turns on the existence of a law of nations, a few clarifications are in order. First of all, what is known as the law of nations is not primarily a written code; it consists for the most part of convention, custom, and common usage. Hence it contains a great deal in addition to fundamental moral law and is based on the relative adjustment between things with regard to their effect or utility. For example, the common recognition that some actions, even in warfare, transgress civilized limits and constitute a crime against humanity underlay the Nuremberg war trials. Again, the generally respected safety of Red Cross personnel during hostilities or the widespread sense that restrictions must be placed on chemical-biological warfare both derive from a law of nations. Nations do share a number of judgments and practices concerning the effects of their mutual relations, and Kennan himself requires a concept such as the law of nations in order to support his judgments concerning nuclear weapons.

As previously noted, Kennan registered serious doubts about the acceptability of nuclear weapons, but he has equivocated about the terms of his objection. A judgment of expedience merely expresses a functional relation between a thing and a given end. The reader will recall that Kennan defined the purpose of state action as the pursuit of its own interest. There would therefore be nothing inherently immoral about the use of nuclear weapons, even in a preventive attack, if they in fact successfully secured the self-interest of a state. He has said that the true end of diplomacy, to change men's hearts, cannot be achieved by nuclear weapons. On these terms alone nuclear weapons can only be judged inexpedient, not necessarily immoral. To contend that our national interest calls for inducing others, as pacifically as possible, to consent to our objectives does not place any intrinsic limitation on the effective attainment of that interest. Kennan did, however, raise a moral criticism of nuclear war in a lecture he delivered over the BBC a year after the Reith Lectures. He condemned nuclear war as inherently immoral because it threatened to destroy human existence, a consideration that transcended national interest. The use of these weapons seemed to him

> wrong in the old-fashioned meaning of the term. It involves an egocentricity on our part that has no foundation either in religious faith or in political philosophy. It accords poorly with the view we like to take of ourselves as people whose lives are founded on a system of spiritual and ethical values. We of this generation did not create the civilization of which we are a part and, only too obviously, it is not we who are destined to complete it. We are not the owners of the planet we inhabit; we are only its custodians. There are limitations on the extent to which we should be permitted to devastate or pollute it. Our own safety and convenience is not the ultimate of what is at stake in the judgment of these problems. People did not struggle and sacrifice over the course of several thousand years to produce this civilization merely in order to make it possible for us, the contemporaries of 1959, to make an end to it or to place it in jeopardy at our pleasure for the sake of our personal safety. Our deepest obligation . . . [relates] not to ourselves alone but to the past and to the future. [62]

It would be helpful to know more exactly what Kennan means by morally "wrong" in the "old-fashioned" sense. He does suggest here, though, the existence of a natural moral law, expressed in part through the law of nations, which measures and limits the purposes as well as the methods of states and which provides rational criteria of right and wrong for both political and personal life.

Kennan's argument for the divorce of ethics and diplomacy rests partially on the premise that governmental action is an amoral activity; as a result, the moral standards of personal life do not apply to governments, which are not proper *situs* of responsibility. Strictly speaking, political action, accordingly, is not truly human action:

> A government is an agent, not a principal; and no more than any other agent may it attempt to be the conscience of its principal. In particular, it may not subject itself to those supreme laws of renunciation and self-sacrifice that represent the culmination of individual moral growth. Morality, then, as the channel to individual self-fulfillment—yes. Morality as the foundation of civic virtue, and accordingly as a conditon precedent to successful democracy—yes. Morality in governmental method, as a matter of conscience and preference on the part of our people—yes. But morality as a general criterion for measuring and comparing the behavior of different states—no. Here other criteria, sadder, more limited, more practical, must be allowed to prevail. [63]

Admittedly, government is not subject to the law of love and to the counsels of perfection as individuals are; its purpose is the lesser, but still noble one of securing peace and justice among its own citizens and, in the wider society of nations, of protecting its legitimate interests and promoting peace among peoples. Political particularism, the limitation of moral principles to relations among one people, leads to the barbarization of relations between peoples just as certainly as the restriction of morality to the personal level tends finally to its dissolution altogether and a corrosion of civic virtue. Modern bourgeois society has experienced the latter fate. Do we need another holocaust to demonstrate the result of the tribalization of morality? Persons, not institutions, make judgments and perform actions. One would expect to find Kennan, given his aversion to the bureaucratization and depersonalization of modern life, reluctant to propagate the pernicious myth of impersonal, and hence irresponsible, action. Kennan's position, furthermore, does not fit his view of the public's role in foreign policy. Time and again he has inveighed against the intrusion of public opinion upon policy-making. He decries what he calls America's democratic "diplomacy by dilettantism," insisting on the need for a professional élite to guide the people in the field of foreign affairs and to assume independent responsibility for the conduct of diplomacy. Perhaps, though, Kennan really believes that foreign policy ought to serve a larger end than national aggrandizement. At the beginning of *Realities of American Foreign Policy* he vaguely intimates that "the conduct of foreign relations ought not to be conceived as a purpose in itself for a political society, and particularly a democratic society, but rather as one of the means by which some higher and more comprehensive purpose is pursued."[64]

Although Kennan has tried to curtail moralism in foreign relations by advocating an amoral pursuit of national self-interest, he himself has not escaped moralism. On numerous occasions he passes moral judgment, and he has even spoken of a "higher law morality." In a speech before he left the State Department he declared that nowhere in the world did the idea that state power is evil, with the corollary that political acts are exempt from moral standards, seem more deeply rooted than in Russia. He expressed confidence, however, that with the passage of time Soviet political ruthlessness would diminish: "Individual moral concepts cannot remain permanently separable from the problem of how man treats man within the framework of state power."[65] A few years later, when Soviet power began to crack in Eastern Europe, Kennan remarked in an interview with Joseph Alsop that "these events do have grandeur, because they are visible proof that certain principles, certain moral principles, really must be observed in the long run in the successful government of great peoples. These events prove that if those principles are constantly violated over a long period of time, this violation avenges itself."[66] Kennan submitted that certain moral principles were objective and immutable; they were not man-made: "They were there. God created them, in my opinion."[67] While Kennan's first statement bore on a state's action within its own boundaries, his second remark pertained to Russia's satellite diplomacy, which it seems arbitrary to separate from his general view of the relation between diplomacy and ethics.

One does not normally expect a realist to be squeamish about sin, but Kennan dismays us. In the *Memoirs* he recalls how Harry Hopkins consulted him on what the United States should do about Russia's seizure of Poland at the end of the war. Kennan sternly responded that the United States should not even recognize what was happening. As he recollects the exchange:

Hopkins: "Then you think it's just sin," he said, "and we should be agin it."
Kennan: "That's just about right," I replied.
Hopkins: "I respect your opinion," he said, sadly. "But I am not at liberty to accept it."[68]

For a man with a tragic sense of life Kennan has an exceptionally strong indisposition to treat with evil. He objected to the Ramsay MacDonald government's official recognition of the Soviet Union, feeling that at most a tacit association with evil is tolerable:

Even in personal life, we do not have the luxury of being able to ignore evil entirely. We all have to make our compromises with the Devil, and to have our dealings with him. But personally, I have always liked to think of my own relations with the Devil as being of a *de facto*, rather than a *de jure*, nature.[69]

His warm approval of Woodrow Wilson's flat refusal to recognize the Soviet Union does not go so far as to consort with evil even in a *de facto* manner. "This was a hard position," Kennan writes in a Wilsonian spirit, "and a negative one. But it was one based squarely on principle." [70]

Kennan's selective morality bestows certain prerogatives on the United States that Russia does not enjoy. Periodically in the *Memoirs* Kennan indignantly chastises Russia for acting according to her national interest during the war. But he does not stop with a rebuke of Russian realism. When Kennan sees the mote in another's eye, he forgets the beam in his own. Pressing for the partition of Germany and discouraging economic cooperation with Russia in 1945, he sentimentally wrote:

> The motives for which the Russians might be expected to interest themselves in UNRRA (United Nations Relief and Reconstruction Agency) would have little in common, it seemed to me, with the general altruistic interest in European reconstruction by which our people were motivated: the Soviet leaders would use their participation in this organization primarily for political purposes, and would do what they could to see that relief was distributed in such a way as to benefit their political cause. [71]

Kennan's attitudes toward Hitler and Stalin, Nazi Germany and Soviet Russia, illustrate his moral arbitrariness. Kennan justifiably condemns the maniacal Stalin, whom he describes as emerging from the criminal fringe of the Communist party. He has not a good word for the homicidally paranoid Stalin. Hitler too Kennan considers an evil man, but he muses that if "evil can be great, then the quality of greatness cannot, I think, be denied him." [72] One would not have to diminish Stalin's evil in order to deal equably with Hitler. But Soviet Russia always represented, if not unmitigated evil, a greater evil to Kennan than Nazi Germany. He seems never to have been able pragmatically to curb his animus toward the Russian evil. Russia never made a fit associate for the West in Kennan's eyes. Complicity with her against Germany, he remonstrates, "meant that as early as the late 1930's, no clean, moral victory for the West was any longer in the cards—no victory in the name of priciples and ideals." [73] More than once Kennan has gone as far as to suggest that it might have been Russia's bad manners—her traits of secrecy, duplicity, and greediness—that were responsible for the fanatical Nazi hatred toward her and the Nazi campaign of annihilation in the East. [74]

George Kennan proposed the doctrine of realism to replace a democratic idealism that ignored the factors of self-interest and power in international relations. On inspection, the realist criticism of American diplomacy suffers from its own naiveté, for it neglects the convenient union between idealism and self-interest. As Herbert Butterfield has observed, "We forget how easy it is to be virtuous when the cause of virtue is one with our interests and provides concealment for them." [75] American foreign policy has not stumbled along on illusion, blunder, and inadvertence; in light of America's steady and successful pursuit of her own interest, the realist counsel seems gratuitous. Kennan believed that idealism had engendered a fearful, self-defeating messianism in American diplomacy. As an alternative he proffered a candid and sober pragmatism. Strictly construed, Kennan's political realism defines the object of diplomacy as the pursuit of the national self-interest and renders legitimate any means that expediently serve that purpose. Such a policy does not actually succeed in placing any restraint on national action, except that of utility. Despite his profession, Kennan does not, in fact, exclude moral judgments from his thinking. Moralism poses no obstacle to the pursuit of self-interest, nor, as Kennan shows, does the realistic pursuit of self-interest provide any guarantee against moralism. George Kennan is a moralist, but his moralism contravenes the doctrine of realism.

Men cannot avoid making moral judgments because human activity is moral activity; as long as men retain their humanity they will continue to exercise moral judgments. In neither the personal nor the political dimension of human existence need men disregard their legitimate interests; in both dimensions the determination of those interests requires rational standards of moral conduct. A reasonable, decent concern for *legitimate* interests presupposes that we know the nature of man and the purpose of society. Without this knowledge we will necessarily have something other than a human life, and quite possibly we shall not have life at all. The concept of political realism, as presented by George Kennan, fails to reveal the realities of political life or furnish the ground for a genuinely human politics. Shortly after the first Great War of this century the French essayist Julien Benda described the era's pragmatic cult of realism as "one of the most remarkable turning points in the moral history of the human species." [76] Writing in 1928, Benda proved to be prescient, for he felt that this was not an adventitious phenomenon: "The political realism of the 'clerks,' far from being a superficial fact due to the caprice of an order of men, seems to me bound up with the very essence of the modern world." [77] It is symptomatic of our time that the more we have claimed to uncover political reality, the less human politics has become.

3

The Christian Realism of Reinhold Niebuhr

PRIOR TO THE SECOND WORLD WAR REINHOLD NIEBUHR CONTRIB-
uted an autobiographical sketch to the *Christian Century* in
which he stated that about midway in his ministry he "under-
went a fairly complete conversion of thought which involved
rejection of almost all the liberal theological ideals and ideas
with which I ventured forth in 1915." [1] Munich was the
capstone to experiences that led him to "conclude that the
whole of contemporary history proves that liberal culture has
not seen the problem of mankind in sufficient depth to
understand its own history. Its too simple moralism has
confused issues at almost every turn." [2] In the crucible of World
War I, a lost peace, depression, and industrial strife, Reinhold
Niebuhr rejected the liberal philosophy he had inherited and
formulated what came to be known as Christian realism.

The liberalism, secular and religious alike, that Niebuhr
abandoned encompassed not merely an economic or social

theory but the entire view of human nature and history that underlay those theories. [3] Indeed, he lost faith in human nature itself, faith in the essential goodness and wisdom of man and in the progressive movement of history. Whether expressed in the Christian social gospel's reliance upon individual moral suasion or the secular faith in the potentiality of scientific reason, liberalism represented "a kind of blindness to which those are particularly subject who imagine that their intelligence has emancipated them from all the stupidities of the past. . . . Liberalism is not only a form of blindness. It is a blindness difficult to cure, because it is a disease among classes who imagine themselves particularly clear-eyed." [4] Its chief, bankrupt tenets were the following: that injustice, a result of ignorance, will recede before education; that the forward march of civilization makes it wrong to challenge gradualness; that the character of individuals, not social systems, guarantees justice; that appeals to love and brotherhood will ultimately prevail; that goodness brings happiness and that an awareness of this will overcome human selfishness; and that wars arise from the tragic errors of stupid people.

Niebuhr's pastoral experience in the strike-ridden Detroit of the 1920s convinced him that neither religious nor secular liberals took a hard and full enough view of human nature, thereby failing to appreciate the ineradicable element of egoism in all human action. Man was an inherently self-regarding creature; since individuals could barely transcend the taint of self-interest to achieve a degree of mutuality in personal relations, social groups could never do so. Niebuhr shared John Dewey's socialist criticism of the New Deal, but Dewey symbolized the modern rationalist error of believing that time and the proper pedagogy would liberate the human mind and eliminate social problems. The rationalist "cultural lag" theory, that education will gradually free intelligence so as to enable men to see social affairs harmoniously, prescinded from actual experience. This notion, wrote Niebuhr, "does not perceive the perennial and inevitable character of the subordination of reason to interest in the social struggle." [5] Hence a state of perpetual warfare existed in politics wherein power must be pitted against power. In the manifesto of his radical pessimism, *Moral Man and Immoral Society*, Niebuhr depicted the intractability of collective self-interest and the resulting, ineluctable social struggle:

> What is lacking among all these moralists, whether religious or rational, is an understanding of the brutal character of the behavior of all human collectivities, and the power of self-interest and collective egoism in all inter-group relations. Failure to recognize the stubborn resistance of group egoism to all moral and inclusive social objectives inevitably involves them in unrealistic and confused political thought. They regard social conflict either as an impossible method of achieving morally approved ends or as a momentary expedient which a more perfect education or a purer religion will make unnecessary. They do not see that the limitations of the human imagination, the easy subservience of reason to prejudice and passion, and the consequent persistence of irrational egoism, particularly in group behavior, make social conflict an inevitability in human history, probably to its very end. [6]

Liberals cannot recognize the necessity of power and coercion in order to achieve social cohesion and cooperation. Yet the exercise of power inescapably creates injustice and perpetuates political warfare because those who organize power always arrogate to themselves inordinate privilege. The intrinsically coercive nature of politics, therefore, renders forceful methods morally neutral. "Politics will," Niebuhr concluded, "to the end of history, be an area where conscience and power meet, where the ethical and coercive factors of human life will interpenetrate and work out their tentative and uneasy compromises." [7] To the Christian realist of *Moral Man and Immoral Society*, the question of means and ends in politics raised essentially pragmatic considerations and posed a technical rather than ethical problem. Immediate effects would have to be weighed against ultimate ones, and no political action could be discounted as inherently immoral; in fact, "there is no moral value which may be regarded as absolute." [8] Niebuhr's answer to the means/end problem in politics led him to a radically utilitarian recipe of breaking eggs to make historical omelets:

> Once we have made the fateful concession of ethics to politics, and accepted coercion as a necessary instrument of social cohesion, we can make no absolute distinctions between non-violent and violent types of coercion or between coercion used by governments and that which is used by revolutionaries. If such distinctions are made they must be justified in terms of the consequences in which they result. The real question is: what are the political possibilities of establishing justice through violence? [9]

Holding justice as the proximate ethical norm of any particular political action, Niebuhr separated the morality of the end from the nature of the means employed to secure it, and he implied that success determined the justified use of force. A fair chance for success comprises one legitimate element of prudential judgments, but without a fuller understanding of prudence Niebuhr's pragmatic calculation merely rationalized ruthlessness. Moreover, given the radically tainted perspective of every self-interested individual and group, Niebuhr precluded an objective delineation of the goal of justice itself. If passion and interest enslave all men equally, then one vision of justice is as warped as another.

During the 1930s radical socialism provided the standard of justice for Niebuhr. In 1935 the Fellowship of Socialist Christians, to which he belonged, founded *Radical Religion* as a journal devoted to uniting Christianity and Marxist political philosophy. Desiring Christianity to shed its liberal-bourgeois identification, the Fellowship saw in Marxism a prophetic view of history that Christianity must recapture "to be truly effective in our era." [10] As a Christian, Niebuhr rejected Marxist materialism and determinism, but he also forswore a moralism that relied on good will to obtain justice. Like Marxists, Niebuhr declared, "we believe that a capitalist society is destroying itself and yet that it must be destroyed, lest it reduce, in the delirium of its disintegration, our whole civilization to barbarism." [11] In America and elsewhere social ownership of the means of production could be won only through struggle, and in the conflict Christianity must array itself on the side of the workingman. Moralists naively believed that good men could achieve justice within any social order; a realistic radical, however, need not believe that socialism would abolish human egoism and injustice. Socialism merely sought institutions that would diminish disproportions of power and increase society's equilibrium. [12]

Enlisting Christianity into the service of radical socialism compelled Niebuhr to strike a delicate balance between opposing positions. He defined Christian radicalism as "the application of prophetic religious insights to life and the world." [13] Christian radicalism thus rejected both a spiritualism that depreciated the importance of temporal existence and a naturalism that found sufficient explanation of human life in history. A pessimism that neglected urgent social tasks was as unacceptable as a utopianism that thought it would solve the whole human problem through political and economic reorganization. Pessimists who denied the image of God in man were as perverse as optimists who forgot man's fallen nature. Religious individualists who ignored the social order, or relied on good will for change, or wistfully desired a sacral society were as misguided as radicals who assumed that a new society would eliminate evil and strife. Niebuhr joined Christianity and socialism in a dialectical, biblical view of life that "affirms the meaning of history and of man's natural existence on the one hand, and on the other hand insists that the centre, source and fulfillment of history lie beyond history." [14]

Throughout the decade Niebuhr allied with socialist opponents of the New Deal, such as John Dewey and Norman Thomas, who did not share his theological stance. Critical of the New Deal for not instituting the basic structural changes that he believed modern capitalist economy required, Niebuhr regarded its inability to prevent the renewal of depression in 1937 as indicative of Roosevelt's unpragmatic, unsound centrism. [15] The tenant relief program subsidizing individual farmers, for example, typified the New Deal's inherent flaw, for it did "not challenge the basic individualism of our present economy." [16] Agricultural technology and the modern market had made individual farming an anachronism.

> The alternative cannot be between individual farming and corporate farming. The alternative is between cooperative farming and capitalistic corporate farming. . . . We cannot choose whether or no we want collectivism. The machine has decided that for us, for good or ill. The question is whether we want capitalistic or cooperative collectivism. [17]

Roosevelt's pump-priming policy of credit-manipulation, government spending, and wages and hours acts was preferable to the policy of his reactionary foes, even though it "reveals how impossible it is to heal the ills of modern capitalism within the presuppositions of capitalism itself." [18]

Once hoping for a new mass party that would include both Socialists and Communists, Niebuhr greeted the CIO as an invigorating radical impetus to the labor movement. He lamented the decline of the Socialist party and hoped that the CIO would not surrender the radical vision of a new society for trade unionism's paltry benefits. [19] As late as 1939 Niebuhr still condemned the New Deal for failing to initiate fundamental reforms that would redistribute wealth.

The Rooseveltian doctors are quacks only in the sense that they hold out the prospect of an ultimate recovery which lies completely beyond the potency of their medicine. This quackery must be recognized and exposed. It must also be recognized that the spending solution gradually excludes other possible, and possibly more fundamental, solutions. [20]

Like many American intellectuals during the 1930s, Niebuhr admired Communism's "great experiment," until the Soviet purges and finally the Nazi-Soviet nonaggression pact shattered their dream. In 1940 *Radical Religion,* under Niebuhr's editorship, was less militantly renamed *Christianity and Society;* hitherto he had distinguished sharply between Fascism and Communism, viewing the latter as essentially harmonious with the spirit of Christianity. "Succinctly stated, nationalism is a pre-prophetic religion and Communism is a form of secularized prophecy." [21] Niebuhr preferred the universal goal of prophetic religion, where all men shared in the new creation, to the particularism of tribal religion; moreover, Communism had a vision of an eternally peaceful, just world. [22] Admittedly Communism, like Fascism, had a demonology, but "it does not, at least, identify the principle of evil with a certain race but only with *the bearers of a particular form of social organization.* . . . Communism may be a corruption of prophetic religion, but it is not its antithesis." [23] The decadent primitivism of Fascism "is a worse fate than the natural and robust primitivism of Russia, in which there are genuine seeds of a high culture," [24] Though he harbored reservations about Marxism's claims for the unlimited capacity of intelligence unfettered by religion, Niebuhr found the morally obtuse pessimism of orthodox Christianity and the simple moral optimism of liberal Christianity more unpalatable. If Marxism's utopianism and naturalism remained alien to Christianity, Marxism correctly revealed how interest corrupts all human action, how injustice results from disproportionate social power, and how justice ensues necessarily from social struggle. [25] For a time Niebuhr thought Marxism's conception of justice and its anthropology separable, and he ignored the full implications of its revolutionary doctrine.

As Niebuhr was writing, however, the Communist party purges and Moscow trials began in Russia. By the spring of 1937 news of the trials reached the West and stirred doubts in his mind. Mildly critical and confused at first over the trials' meaning, he retained his faith in "the great Russian experiment," but cautioned American radicals not to expect the kingdom of God on earth: "On the whole what happens there is full of promise to mankind. But why should anyone believe that there are no serpents in this Garden of Eden? We will at least continue to suspect that there are if such dubious apples as the Moscow trials emanate from there." [26]

Niebuhr placed his confidence in the Soviet system, which he judged basically good, and blamed only particular men for untoward deviations. [27] But the trials raised questions about the use of power that he could not evade for long. Responding to a British Christian socialist's whitewash of the trials, Niebuhr warned Christians to be on guard against the realist fallacy "that power is good as long as it is wielded for good purposes, the socialization of economic life for instance. Power is always a source of corruption . . . Christian 'realists' should be saved from the error of ever giving their moral carte blanche to any political overlord, whether he be king or commissar." [28] The army purges of 1937 and the collective farm purges of the following year finally broke the spell of enchantment with the Russian experiment. Niebuhr was now convinced that the democratic process must be preserved in any transition toward socialism. He still affirmed his belief that "Marxism is an essentially correct theory and analysis of the economic realities of modern society," but the stark reality of Stalin's despotism refuted its theory that the state will wither away after capitalism crumbles and that force in society originates in class organization. Assuming that dissent and conflict in a community represent capitalist atavisms, the Soviets "allow the power of their state to grow unduly, vainly imagining that the heart which beats under the tunic of a commissar is of different stuff from the hearts of ancient kings and potentates."[29]

After five years of purges and trials the diplomatic revolution of August 23, 1939, dashed any remaining hope of American radicals in the Russian experiment. The Nazi-Soviet nonaggression pact and the subsequent rape of Poland finally disabused the radicals. Power politics dictated Russia's cynical treachery, Niebuhr recognized, but the betrayal of Communist ideology by Russian nationalism came as "a bitter blow." Niebuhr still did not make clear whether his disillusion lay with the Marxist dream itself or merely with its embodiment. [30] At any rate, Russia's *coup de maître* in power politics created an embarrassing problem for the political realist. Niebuhr now felt that thoroughgoing opportunism was as inadequate as simple moralism in politics. Except for the purists everyone realized that politics always involves a power struggle. Power alone did not suffice, however, for the real issue lay "in the relation of national interests to the universal values which transcend a nation." [31] Russian nationalism had corrupted a transcendent value. Within a few years Niebuhr feared that Russian national self-interest insufficiently restrained a Marxist ideal he had come to regard as demonic.

From an early date Niebuhr believed a second general war in Europe inevitable. When Italy conquered Ethiopia and Germany occupied the Rhineland in 1936, he reflected that "there are tides in history which move by inexorable force and there are floods which can be dammed, but not prevented." [32] Thus far he perceived no angels in the conflict, and he did not favor American involvement. He thought that the United States should temporarily balance a policy of collective security with one of neutrality, though this was a precarious balance. "These endless relativities of pragmatic politics," he stated, "prove both the necessity of a religiously oriented pacifism and the peril of mixing such a pacifism with pragmatic politics. . . . All governments fight sin with sin." It is a dangerous but, he added, "necessary procedure." [33]

Prior to Munich Niebuhr supported the imposition of economic sanctions upon Germany, condemning capitalists in England and America who held the economic power but declined to halt Fascism because they liked Communism less. [34] The United States and Britain, he warned, would not act until Germany threatened their imperial interests; hence, people should not be fooled later "by pure imperialism hiding behind the facade of collective security for democracy." [35] He criticized isolationists on several grounds: they did not foresee the economic dislocation that the United States would suffer if she stayed out of the next war; they allied, in spite of themselves, with nationalists who endorsed isolation for different reasons; and they underestimated the probability of America's entanglement in the approaching war. Advocates of collective security, on the other hand, could not admit its past failure and refrained from employing the economic sanctions that might be effective. The next war, he expected, would hardly be one that "any decent person can sanction." [36] Niebuhr found it difficult to approve collective security, since others often promoted it as a means of protecting Russia. Pragmatically, the West should force Russia to fend for herself:

We fully appreciate the solid achievements of Russian economy but we have strong doubts about the wholesomeness of politics in Russia. We are not willing to see young Americans die to protect Stalin's type of dictatorship from Hitler's type of dictatorship. Now don't accuse us of equating them. We still believe there are important differences. But the similarities have been growing. But whatever the differences or similarities they are not worth a world war. Therefore we find ourselves inclining to abstention not as a matter of absolute pacifist principle but as a matter of immediate policy.[37]

After Munich the choice between international anarchy or capitulation to barbarism became less equivocal. Munich represented not only the treason of the Western capitalist oligarchy but a cultural and spiritual malady in democratic society, which ran deeper than its socioeconomic organization.[38] Niebuhr had previously shared Socialists' doubts about the justifiability of modern war and about radicalism's chances for surviving another world war,[39] but by late 1939 he thought war not only inevitable but clearly preferable to Nazi tyranny.[40]

As this second general war drew closer, Niebuhr forcefully argued the Christian case against pacifism. In an essay entitled "Why the Christian Church Is Not Pacifist" Niebuhr explained that the church did not support pacifism because it did not equate the Gospel with the law of love, for Christianity takes into account not only the norm of love but also the fact of sin. The Gospel's good news announces not the law of love but the revelation of divine mercy for man's self-love. Because men are sinners justice can be achieved only through coercion and resistance to coercion; hence, war is inevitable. All historical judgments are relative and ambiguous; nevertheless, we must make them, and in the present situation it would be "sheer moral perversity to equate the inconsistencies of a democratic civilization with the brutalities which modern tyrannical states practice."[41]

Niebuhr commended the pacifist fidelity to love as the ultimate moral norm of life, maintaining that men most closely approximate love on earth by a justice achieved through a balance of power where every life and interest is protected against all others. All life "is an expression of power," and the relation of one life to another resembles that of one power to another because "each life seeks as its own, something which is equally required by other life." [42] Christian pacifists erred insofar as they failed to recognize that a pure act of sacrifice can occur only outside history in eternity, that "the Cross is not an instrument of social policy." [43] Within history men must settle for conflict and a tolerable balance of power; perfect love at once fulfills and negates human history. Pacifists, as a result of their misplaced faith, either make no moral judgments or accept tyranny rather than face the temporary anarchy of war; a true Christian faith "sees the whole of human history as involved in guilt, and finds no release from guilt except in the grace of God." [44] Christians, then, ought always to remember the evil in their good; yet this will lead them to inaction only if they are seeking an illusory, sinless position in history. [45]

His repudiation of pacifism did not alter Niebuhr's noninterventionist position during 1940. A facile moral choice either for or against intervention he deemed unrealistic; instead, the security of American interests must determine the decision. As Holland, Belgium, and France fell, Niebuhr grew alarmed at the prospect of a possible Nazi victory and declared America's moral allegiance to the Allied cause. Yet, while he favored easing restrictions in order to permit more supplies to flow to the Allies, he opposed active American involvement. Moralists failed to understand the basis for American neutrality—"the fact that American vital interests are not imperiled in the conflict." [46] The war bred a crisis of the ultimate order. Nazi barbarism menaced civilization itself, for Hitler's goals "represent a peril to every established value of a civilization which all the Western nations share and of which we are all the custodians." [47] But Niebuhr separated the moral issue from the pragmatic question of strategic policy. Everyone could agree on the moral urgency of a Nazi defeat; despite this fact, the role the United States should play in providing assistance "is a question," he wrote in *Christianity and Society,* "which this journal regards as matters of policy and not of principle." [48] When the Russo-German marriage of convenience abruptly ended in 1941, Niebuhr chastised sentimentalists who opposed our new strategic alliance with Russia. Forgetting his bitter denunciation of Stalin's *Realpolitik* in 1939, Niebuhr insisted that idealism must not be permitted to restrict "strategic flexibility." [49]

By the time America became irrevocably engaged in the European conflagration, Niebuhr had renounced Marxism, but in the early years of the conflict he remained optimistic that the United States could cooperate with Russia. Until 1944 Niebuhr regarded Russia as a basically conservative national state with which America had a common interest in a stable international order. In contrast to the Communist party, which symbolized spiritual imperialism and global revolution, Stalin stood for the enduring, irenic interests of Russia the nation-state. The international Party presented the main impediment to a peaceful *modus vivendi:* "The primary obstacle to achieving it is found in the relationship between Russia and the remnants of the worldwide Communist Party. Russia, as a nation, is not aggressive. All its internal inclinations will be for the maintenance of peace and the status quo after the war." [50] Niebuhr suggested that Stalin, as a gesture of good will, disband the Party in the Anglo-Saxon countries after the war. He continued to believe that if Communism represented a heresy, at least, unlike the anti-Christian nihilism of Nazism, it was guilty of a Christian heresy. "We can come to terms with the one, but not with the other." [51]

Marxism no longer seemed a tenable doctrine to him. National loyalties had undercut its internationalism, "the complexities of history" had refuted its theory of class struggle, capitalism had withstood its predictions, and human nature proved resistent to its narrow, rigid categories. The social struggle for justice would continue, but "democracy will be best served if the illusions and errors of Marxism, which needlessly complicated the struggle, are disavowed and their refutation by historical fact is generously admitted." [52] Niebuhr denounced American liberals' pusillanimity toward Communist policy, and he called upon his fellow churchmen to "have done with 'fellow-travelling' particularly in the church." [53] On the other hand, he chided Americans' myopia and paranoia about the revolutionary ferment in Europe. Postwar Europe would inevitably drift leftward and maintain closer ties with Russia than America. It must be remembered

> that Russia has tremendous advantages over us in the game of Europe. . . . Europe is bound to be radical. It is rather sad that the wealthy democracies will try to build Europe in their image. It can not be done. . . . Europe will have to work out its own salvation with not too much aid from either Russia or the West; but with a more intimate relation with Russia than with us. [54]

Although he considered a third world war intolerable, especially in view of Europe's natural leftward tendency, Niebuhr later expressed the reservation that "it must be conceded that there is always the possibility that we may pay too high a price for Russian cooperation by delivering Europe into her hands." [55] The contours of the postwar order remained vague, but at this stage the potential conflict between East and West looked as if it would be limited to the pragmatic level of power politics.

A reassessment of the conception of human nature and society, which *Moral Man and Immoral Society* set forth in 1932, accompanied Niebuhr's shifting attitude toward Marxism in the forties. *The Children of Light and the Children of Darkness,* published in 1944, marked a significant departure from his former pessimism and its radical implications. The neoorthodox theological underpinning of Niebuhr's political theory did not change, [56] but he now attached to it the liberal theory of pluralism. The new analysis and judgment of liberal-democratic society contained in this work provided the political catechism for a younger generation of American liberals. *The Children of Light and the Children of Darkness* presaged the celebration of American liberal capitalism in which a political economy of countervailing power formed the correlate of moral countervailance. Pluralistic democratic politics, Niebuhr contended, excluded fundamental social change and the use of force in the political struggle; yet the democratic pluralism he outlined for postwar American liberalism did not entail an equally consensual and pacific American role in the world community.

Never an optimist, Niebuhr now feared that complete pessimism culminated in political absolutism, although an unqualified pessimism should preclude rule by the one as well as by the many. The Pascalian view of human nature suited a democratic society better than either moral optimism or cynicism. The paradox of democracy consisted in the fact that "man's capacity for justice makes democracy possible; but man's inclination to injustice makes democracy necessary." [57] The children of darkness are the moral cynics who recognize no law beyond their own self-will and interest, while the children of light "believe that self-interest should be brought under the discipline of a higher law." [58] The children of light have built democratic civilization, but now the shrewder children of darkness threaten their work:

> The children of light have not been as wise as the children of darkness. . . . It must be understood that the children of light are foolish not merely because they underestimate the power of self-interest among the children of darkness. They underestimate this power among themselves. [59]

Modern secularism, in both its bourgeois and Marxist manifestations, had optimistically rejected the doctrine of original sin. A sound political theory, maintained Niebuhr, must be based on the recognition that "there is no level of human moral or social achievement in which there is not some corruption of inordinate self-love." [60] As a result, modern secular idealism sought the source of political conflict in environment and social organization rather than in human nature itself, forgetting that man has a will to power, as well as a capacity for selflessness, which sets him eternally in opposition to his fellows. The children of light must learn the wisdom of, but remain free from, the children of darkness.

Democratic society, according to Niebuhr, was both the cause and the effect of social and moral pluralism. Catholic natural-law theory, secular rationalism, and nihilism all inadequately dealt with the problem of diversity in the modern world. Only a deep religious humility, which challenges every pretension to truth, and strong democratic institutions, which check every power with a countervailing power, can mitigate the social conflict and preserve the toleration vital to modern, pluralistic society.

The good society in Niebuhr's reformulation of Christian realism emerged as the most neutrally counterpoised one. For Niebuhr and a generation of liberals then coming of age the modern era inaugurated "the gradual ascendancy of politics over economics," [61] that is, the managed adjustment between competing group interests within an accepted economic framework. Niebuhr no longer believed that the economy required basic structural change. The welfare and fiscal reforms of the New Deal fashioned a new political society, "a more self-conscious and a more conscious society than economic society. Thus the eternal conflict between the privileged and the poor will be lifted to a new level of consciousness in the postwar period." [62]

Before the United States entered World War II Niebuhr anticipated a new American role in the world during the postwar reconstruction. Looking ahead in 1943, he proposed basing the postwar international order upon a joint Russo-Anglo-Saxon world hegemony with Britain playing the role of broker in the great-power triumvirate. Citing "the more historical and organic approach to political reality," which he called the British genius, Niebuhr declared that "the world-community of nations must grow. It cannot be manufactured. A global alliance which wins a global war must be the nucleus of a world-wide community of nations. The hegemonous nations in that alliance must create the core of power from which the order-creating authority must be derived." [63] Because of the uneven distribution of power a Russo-Anglo-Saxon world hegemony did not hold out the prospect of immediate justice, but idealists always disregarded the unity that must precede justice. The establishment of justice depended upon a durable international order, and that order must correspond to the actualities of power. A realistic plan for international peace and justice must proceed on the understanding that "the basis of world order must be laid, not in some abstract world constitution which will not really engage the sense of responsibility of the large powers, but in a partnership of power. Power and responsibility must be made commensurate in the new world order, in a way the League of Nations was unable to accomplish." [64] Charting the path between a great-power imperialism and a quixotic international equalitarianism called for the awareness that "all political tasks require a shrewd admixture of principles and expediency; of loyalty to genuine standards of justice and adjustment to the actual power political realities of the given moment." [65]

This trusteeship's fate clearly hinged on Russian-American relations, particularly their relations in Europe's political vacuum. Underlining the strategic importance of European organization, Niebuhr warned that the Continent must "not become either a Russian or an Anglo-Saxon colony, or a cockpit for the rival power impulses of the great powers, nor yet a mere tool of the combined politics of the great powers." [66] This meant, Niebuhr argued in 1943 and 1944, an economically unified European federation with the socialization of property. Europe must forge her own destiny without Russia's or America's interference; America's prime responsibility rested in creating a viable and permanent United Nations. [67] "The real peril to the world community," he wrote, "comes from the adolescent sense of power in Russia and America, two nations, ideologically so different and yet in many respects so similar." [68] Niebuhr feared a nascent American imperialism: "Isolationism is dead; but American imperialism is rising." [69]

For the war's remainder Niebuhr claimed that only a Russo-Anglo-Saxon triumvirate could insure a stable peace; accordingly, he felt that the United States should do everything possible to preserve a mutuality of interest between Russia and the West. He defended the United Nations proposals against those who desired a purer world government, conceding that the Dumbarton Oaks plan created a great-power alliance rather than a true world government. Modern technology compelled nations to seek justice within a context of centralized, concentrated power. Russia plainly intended to establish a security zone in eastern Europe, but her policy, Niebuhr averred, "differs in degree rather than in kind from that of the other great powers. . . . Russia is not driven by the mania of world conquest, though it obviously has residual fears of the Western world." [70] America should not, he urged, intensify those fears.

In 1945 Niebuhr envisioned America as playing a limited, supportive role in Europe. Since the United States did not belong to the European community, injecting herself into Continental affairs would be futile and harmful. America needed to cement relations with Great Britain, though not at the risk of excluding Russia, which "would make a third world war quite inevitable." [71] America should support the democratic socialist center in Europe in order to deprive Russia of opportunity for penetration, but lack of complete accord with Russia must not be allowed to provoke an unthinkable third world war. Russia, Niebuhr affirmed despite his Marxist disaffection, represented a modicum of good, and the Soviet danger did not compare with the Nazi assault on civilization itself. "We have to 'appease' the Russians because a war with Russia means a civil war within the boundaries of civilization." [72]

Niebuhr criticized pro-Russian liberals for refusing to see that Russia could not unify Europe, first, because European conservatives had sufficient strength to withstand her and, second, because Britain and the United States would not permit it. Anti-Russian liberals, for their part, did not recognize how America's economic power, a more covert influence than Russia's and Britain's machinations, threatened international peace. Conscious that isolationist sentiment might revive at the end of the war, Niebuhr emphasized that the European problem could be solved only through economic reconstruction. [73] The barrier to a Russo-American rapprochement was mutual mistrust, a mistrust fed especially by those who considered war a likelihood for which they must prepare. Of the military in particular Niebuhr cautioned: "It is the business of military strategists to prepare for all eventualities; and it is the fatal error of such strategists to create the eventualities for which they prepare." [74]

When the atomic bombing of Japan terminated the war in the Pacific theater, Niebuhr observed that this weapon represented the logical culmination of warfare. The existence of the atomic bomb witnessed to the need for a stable international government in order to safeguard the survival of the species, but chances for a world society were dim. [75] Neither banishment of the bomb nor outlawry of war appeared practical. Atomic knowledge might possibly be exchanged for arbitration of outstanding diplomatic issues, but recent Russian intransigence made this impossible also. Present realities simply did not allow avoidance of graver, more remote dangers:

> The fear of mutual annihilation ought indeed to persuade us that a very radical step is necessary to secure the survival of civilization. But unfortunately ultimate perils, however great, have a less lively influence upon the human imagination than immediate resentments and frictions, however small by comparison. [76]

The American response to victory in the Pacific caused Niebuhr to express certain strictures. He took to task liberal purists who wanted to abolish the imperial house and who were reluctant to accept any peace with Japanese capitalists. This radical policy he found "prompted by a peculiarly dangerous type of 'liberalism' in which the imperial power impulse has become strangely mixed with moral idealism. We will destroy nations in order to make 'democracies' out of them." [77] America had to defeat Japan, but our presence in Asia ought to be as brief and as minimal as possible. Although we can prevent men from wreaking harm and enslavement on others, "we cannot change their hearts by power." [78]

Until late 1946 Niebuhr adhered to the position that Europe must steer an independent course and that while neither America nor Russia ought unduly to sway her, she would naturally gravitate toward Russia. Reorganizing Europe required the creation of a democratic socialist order. [79] While he remained convinced that Russia should have her own way in Eastern Europe, which she rightly considered her security zone, he gradually came to think that the United States must take a resolute stance and help Western Europe resist totalitarianism. The economic rehabilitation needed by Europe to give her a stable political life offered the most effective way of countering Russian subversion. [80] He reiterated the prophetic principle that all struggles between human good and evil pale in righteousness before the divine judgment and reminded readers that the Russian threat did not compare to that of Nazism. [81] An assumption that America held the moral leadership of the world and must rescue it from totalitarianism was arrogant, not to say perilous:

> However dangerous Russian totalitarianism may be, if we allow the world to drift into a position in which war against Russia becomes the only alternative, little of any value in Western, or any other civilization, can survive. [82]

The autumn of 1946 saw Niebuhr shifting his position. Negotiations had broken down over the issue of German reparations, and the military build-up that the United States and Russia were promoting in their respective zones was solidifying the division of Germany. Niebuhr chided Christians and sentimental liberals who did not comprehend the "tragic aspects of human existence" and whose tender scruples unfitted them to grapple with "a foe who exploits every gesture of pure trust by new demands." [83] The United States must thwart a swelling Soviet ambition to dominate all of Europe. Criticizing Secretary of State Byrnes's hard-line foreign policy, Henry Wallace only hastened war by trying too hard to avoid it. On the one hand, then, Niebuhr believed a third world war not worth the cost; on the other hand, he rejected any compromise with the Soviets. "Russian truculence," he stated, "cannot be mitigated by further concessions. Russia hopes to conquer the whole of Europe strategically and ideologically." [84] The growing Russian peril "obsesses the European mind" more than the prospect of war. "Our foreign policy is inadequate, but not because of its firmness. It is inadequate because it is not supported by a creative economic and political policy." [85]

Americans should admit that no real peace exists in the world and gird themselves for a policy of patient firmness in order to block Russia's drive to expand her dominion. Without becoming hysterical, Niebuhr told readers, America must not yield to the implacable enemy.

Responding to criticism that his journal, *Christianity and Crisis*, took too intransigent a posture toward Russia, Niebuhr acknowledged that America was no beacon of democratic justice; this, however, did not allay the fact that the nineteenth-century Marxist dream had become the "nightmare of Russian tyranny" from which free peoples everywhere desired protection. Even though the purity of men's deeds never matches their intentions, they cannot avoid their responsibilities. The Nazi danger had exposed the dilemma of imperfect action in a fallen world; now the Communist challenge presented a similar predicament: "Here we face the same problem of the relation between religious self-criticism and political judgments which we faced in the Nazi crisis." [86] Both enemies left no choice: just as we could not appease the Nazi evil, so we could not appease the Russian evil. Communist suppression of free elections in Rumania in November 1946 and in Poland two months later, together with new Soviet revolutionary activity in Western Europe, moved Niebuhr to reevaluate the Russian threat. Despite differences between Nazi Germany and Soviet Russia, he concluded, both are

> ruled by dictatorships which are insecure and which must persuade their subjects that it is the nation and not the dictatorship which is insecure. Secondly, they are strategically inferior to the forces opposed to them unless they can, by the threat of war, gain the advantages which make war possible. [87]

The United States had to risk war in order to deter the Soviets. Explaining the "middle ground" foreign-policy position of the Americans for Democratic Action, which had been formed in January 1947, Niebuhr wrote, "we do not believe that the unification of Europe under Russian power would make for peace. If Russia came within proximate sight of that goal, there would be war." [88] Communism now acquired the character of Nazism in Niebuhr's mind, and his idea of historical inevitability justified America's redemptive mission. Technological developments had given the United States unchallenged hegemony at the same time that they had made international community a necessity. But community, which presupposed trust, did not exist, and hence world government could not exist. "It is now fairly certain that there will be no stable peace in our generation," [89] Niebuhr observed, adding that history had propelled a woefully unprepared America into leadership against Russian power and Communist ideology.

Destiny made American dominance of Europe a historical given, which Niebuhr translated into a moral imperative: "American power is so dominant in the Western world that every problem in European destiny must wait for its solution upon some American decision." [90] America rightly committed herself with the Truman Doctrine to halting the Russian inundation of the European continent; next she must increase her economic support of Europe. Believing that the stumbling block to Europe's salvation arose from our too individualistic conception of democracy, Niebuhr minimized the implications of economic domination. He felt it possible for America to "restore the economic health of Europe without trying to dictate the political organization of European nations." [91] With the announcement of the Marshall Plan for Europe in June 1947, Niebuhr saw a "turning point in postwar history" forging "a nexus between European and American interests." [92] He upheld the Marshall Plan on grounds of practical self-interest. A humanitarian concern for starving Europeans or a desire to preserve political liberty was commendable, but "we must furnish aid also in the interest of our own economic health." [93] A poor Europe could not buy American goods, he pointed out. Answering clerical criticism of the European Recovery Program's economic motivation and its anti-Russian spirit, Niebuhr replied: "We will let you take care of the absolutes if you will allow us to deal with the relativities and ambiguities of the political order. In that field we are a little more expert than you." [94]

Periodically Niebuhr counseled against using military force to meet a political threat and called for a constructive foreign policy instead of a sterile anti-Communism. He warned that the righteousness of our cause would fade in the calamity of another war. Refusing to imagine bridges where they did not exist, he also exhorted extremists not to outrun history in dividing the world in two.[95] Nevertheless, he claimed that America held a divinely ordained commission. In spite of her psychological unpreparedness and moral faults, America might have to resort to force, though Niebuhr hoped she would do so humbly. "The future of our world literally depends, not on the display of our power (though the use of it is necessary and inevitable), but upon the acquisition of virtues which can develop only in humility." [96] America would exercise her power more condignly if she meekly acknowledged its divine ordination:

> Our power will be used the more justly, if we recognize that our possession of it is not a proof of our virtue. Our possession of it is either an "accident" or it is a gift of grace. It is a gift of grace if we recognize history as a realm of divine providence and not as a series of accidents. [97]

When men perceive their power as historically destined or divinely ordained, they are apt to forfeit restraint and to lose a sense of proportion regarding the enemy. After the collapse of Czechoslovakia and the erection of the Berlin blockade, Niebuhr speculated that America might have to undertake war to defeat an inhuman enemy. Russia had suffered setbacks throughout Europe; therefore, even though she was less prepared for war than we, she was relying on America's lack of resolve to hold firm and fight. America could not afford a loss of prestige in Berlin, and we ought to have learned our lesson about concessions from Hitler:

> In view of the Russian weakness we must be ready to risk war rather than yield to Russian pressure. But we must also refrain from any policy of incitement which comes in the category of "preventive war. . . ." Our object must be to avoid war, but not "at all costs." For to pay too high a price for its avoidance is finally to court the peril of the war in the very effort to avoid it. Here lies the moral dilemma of our age. [98]

Renouncing further concessions to an inhuman foe, Niebuhr advocated a steadfast commitment to containment:

> We cannot afford any more compromises. We will have to stand resolutely at every point in our far-flung lines. The risks involved will tempt us again and again to yield. If we do we will deliver the fainthearted in Europe into the hands of the enemies of mankind and will give new hope to the presently subdued Communist forces of Western Europe. [99]

Although he exaggerated the Communist problem, Niebuhr tried to steer a middle course between an irresolute policy and a reckless messianism. While pressing for a policy of firmness and patience, he sought to temper American self-righteousness and to encourage a modesty of purpose. "Powerful men and nations," he reminded readers, "are in greater peril from their own illusions than from their neighbors' hostile designs." [100] He sensed Europe's dread of American anti-Communist hysteria and her fear that America did not earnestly enough want to avoid war. [101] Niebuhr subsequently adopted an inflated version of containment, despite his recognition of the irony of that policy: "It is one of the ironic aspects of the situation that strategies of defense seem to be, and in a sense are, strategies of expansion from the opposite viewpoint." [102] Niebuhr never seriously questioned America's innocence in the cold war; instead, he merely criticized a national naiveté that tended, he believed, to blunt a sense of practicality and to rationalize self-interest in terms of lofty ideals. He hoped America's Christian heritage would instill a sense of sin and moral ambiguity in the national character. Accordingly, "power ought always to be exercised with a certain uneasiness of conscience." [103] Communism sinned grievously on account of its fanatical spiritual pride. America should learn from the example of Communism, for though fortunately "we do not have a philosophy of life which makes us constitutionally fanatical and self-righteous," [104] we do sometimes celebrate the virtue of our cause too much and alternately sink into too great disillusion.

Men should wield power with an uneasy conscience; yet Niebuhr did not doubt that circumstances called for its determined use. Soviet aggression necessitated the creation of a broad, non-Communist alliance so that the West could give Russia the choice of either entering into collective security or facing such an alliance. Actually, he felt "the second proposal [was] probably the better one." [105] The irreducible disparity between political reality and technological development allowed no other alternative. "Our problem," as Niebuhr saw it, "is that technics have established a rudimentary world community but have not integrated it organically, morally or politically. They have created a community of mutual dependence, but not one of mutual trust and respect." [106] World governmentalists erroneously assumed that they could establish political order by fiat and that it would foster the community which, in fact, must antecede government. In contrast, those who desired to form a world government without Russia would only succeed in driving deeper wedges between East and West. The formation of a Western, non-Communist alliance, concluded Niebuhr, provided the most feasible way of averting conflict and sowing the seeds of community. As he explained, the only realistic hope for peace rested upon a favorable balance of power:

> There is, of course, a possibility that a closer political integration of the non-Communist nations may save the world from war by the creation of an adequate preponderance of power in the west. But such an objective is not to be reached by loftily disavowing "power politics" in favor of "law." [107]

Niebuhr still subscribed to the view that Russia and America represented variations of a common democratic principle. Their conflict constituted a "civil war in the heart of western civilization" between its equalitarian and libertarian strains. This realization combined with a due humility about our cause satisfied the claims of Christian conscience and enhanced the prospect for victory. The Soviets, however, were a "fanatical foe" against whom we struggled to preserve a "civilization which we hold to be preferable to the universal tyranny with which Soviet aggression threatens us." [108] By the early 1950s Niebuhr became convinced that the Communist world was wholly incompatible with ours and that the Soviets bore full responsibility for the cold war. Immediately after the Second World War, he contended,

> the Russians began to make it clear that they divided the world into two camps, an "evil capitalist" and a "good communist" one. . . . It is difficult, but necessary, to recognize that the communist ideology has no resources within it for coming to terms with other systems of thought. It is dogmatic without qualification. It may ultimately yield to the pressure of world history, but it is not likely to be beguiled by any international conference. [109]

Niebuhr no longer believed that any common ground existed between Communism and liberal democracy. He defended liberal democracy not because it promised greater justice or even greater liberty than Communism, but because it stood for moral relativity and political neutrality. Liberal democracy's virtue lay in its rejection of any moral hierarchy and any fixed end in political life:

> No good purpose is served by minimizing the tragedy in which we are involved in our struggle with communism by making ourselves believe for instance that communism is a slightly more equalitarian, and ours a slightly more libertarian, version of a common democratic creed. There may be some initial similarities between liberal and communist utopian illusions; but there are few similarities between a democratic tentativity and modesty in holding to our various beliefs and the communist fanaticism in which a monopoly of power unites with illusory hopes to breed cruelty and hatred. [110]

America must both halt the spread of Communist tyranny and avoid war. In this difficult effort the United Nations might provide modest help. Great disproportions of power hindered acts of trust, but the continued existence of disproportionate power seemed inescapable: "We are in the throes of vast forces beyond the control of any single agency or power." [111]

Although Niebuhr at times identified the Russian challenge as primarily moral and political in nature, [112] he endorsed a military response to that challenge. In the spring of 1949 he acclaimed the NATO mutual security pact under discussion as the "logical capstone of a policy which has been developing ever since we emerged from the second World War as the world's most powerful nation." [113] NATO brought to fruition America's incipient sense of global responsibility. Peace depended, according to the pact's logic, "not so much upon the functions of the United Nations as upon the maintenance of preponderant power in the non-Communist world." [114] Insofar as the United Nations presupposed a nonexistent world community, the pact was necessary because "the European nations desire it." America must always strive to prevent war, not simply win it; thus strategists should keep the pact's deterrent purpose in sight. Niebuhr preferred a flexible military alliance of the West to a formal political association, for the latter would deepen the "chasm between Russia and the West and might destroy the minimal bridge between the two in the United Nations." [115] His response to the churches' cool reception of NATO exemplified Niebuhr's pragmatic separation of ethics and politics: "It must be admitted that the pact deals with strategic questions on which the church need not and perhaps ought not to take an official stand." [116]

Disallowing an official clerical stand on NATO, Niebuhr never indicated whether the churches might legitimately take a position on an issue such as nuclear war. A similar pragmatism informed his reasoning concerning the development of the hydrogen bomb. He admitted both the moral gravity of its use and the threat posed to democracy by the secrecy and security surrounding it, but its justification lay in its power to compel peace. If we did not construct the bomb, the Russians would do so and would thereby be able to coerce America into submission; the bomb's purpose was to prevent its use. [117] Niebuhr's sense of historical inevitability foreclosed consideration of morally qualitative differences in military methods. "Our present situation," he observed, "is a heightened and more vivid explication of the human situation." [118] The irresistibility of history precluded unilateral renouncement of the bomb. Human beings were simply neither good enough nor strong enough to rise to such transcendence. Assuring European readers that America really preferred coexistence to a nuclear holocaust, Niebuhr insisted that only a balance of terror could preserve peace: "It is not possible, for instance, to relieve tension by refusing to go ahead with the development of atomic weapons. Peace is preserved by the fear of these atomic weapons." [119] He compared nuclear deterrence to resisting North Korea's invasion of South Korea. Arguing that the "Korean defense was necessary for the same reason that necessitated development of the hydrogen bomb," [120] he explained that both aimed at discouraging aggression and thereby reducing the prospect of general war.

A divorce between ethics and politics continued to characterize Niebuhr's thought. The essential pragmatism of *Moral Man and Immoral Society* remained intact in his political philosophy; that pragmatism simply served other ends. Niebuhr criticized radicals and conservatives alike for indulging in what he called "religious politics," for failing to understand that "religion deals with life's ultimate ends and meanings, while politics must inevitably strive for proximate ends of life and must use ambiguous means to attain them. Therefore it is dangerous to claim the sanctity of the ultimate for political ends and means." [121] It may be necessary to remind the politically immature, those who are inclined to commit the error of misplaced concreteness, of the difference between religion and politics. As far as it goes, Niebuhr's point makes unexceptionable sense; however, this distinction alone can hardly provide adequate grounds for a political philosophy. Even proximate ends, in order to arrive at them intelligibly, require some standard of justice, and even ambiguous means require a concept of prudence as well as justice, unless one settles for sheer expediency. If religious faith cannot provide a satisfactory concept of justice in a pluralistic society, then we must have some rational standard, but Christian realism does not offer a rational standard of justice either. Realism, as Niebuhr defined it in *Christian Realism and Political Problems*, "denotes the disposition to take all factors in a social and political situation, which offer resistance to established norms, into account, particularly the factors of self-interest and power." [122] Political idealism, in contrast, signifies "loyalty to moral norms and ideals, rather than to self-interest, whether individual or collective." [123] Now, as he defined these positions, no necessary contradiction exists between them. Prudence, in fact, dictates that one take cognizance of all existential factors in order duly to adjust moral norms to specific cases. Who will deny the utility of taking a comprehensive and measured view of any problem? Looking at the issue another way, Niebuhr surely was not suggesting one should treat unalloyed self-interest and power as moral norms. If he meant merely that the real, imperfect world in which men live never fully satisfies their best instincts and highest aspirations, he would be stating a truism that does not require religious faith to grasp. Presenting the problematic relation among religion, ethics, and political life in this fashion, Niebuhr created a false antithesis, which rendered both faith and reason irrelevant to politics.

At the same time he was reformulating the doctrine of Christian political realism, Niebuhr took a revised view of Communism, one that significantly transformed the nature of the cold war. The "religious" character of Communism now loomed larger in his thinking; as a result he shifted the cold war from the practical arena of power politics to a more intractable, ideological level. Idealists, he granted, justly criticized an over-reliance upon military power; yet they did not comprehend the special evil of a "political religion":

> They cannot bring themselves to believe in the reality of the evil we face in a fanatic creed of this kind. They cannot imagine a political religion so consistent in its dogmatism that it is able to discount in advance any approach which varies from its dogmas. It is tragic that the yearnings of a whole world for peace should be thwarted by such intransigence. But there it is. We serve no useful purpose by obscuring this cruel fact in sentimentalities and illusions. [124]

He attributed the demonic quality of Communism to its pretension that the proletarian revolution constitutes a trans-historical force from which arises an irresistible tendency to play God in history. Communism had not only severed its kinship with Western democracy, but it had lost its moorings in traditional Russian nationalism. Giving this focus to the Russian challenge substituted the more obdurate dimension of ideology and morality for a realist emphasis on self-interest and power. Communism's surrogate religion, its dogmatism and pseudo-science, and its unchecked monopoly of power made it even more dangerous than Nazism. [125] Just as liberal democracy was more righteous than Nazism, our cause was so much worthier than the Soviet Union's that Niebuhr feared that a complacent self-esteem might overtake America. [126]

Implacable in her dogmatism, Russia varied her weapons of assault, so Niebuhr called for tactical flexibility. If Russian expansion took the form of political subversion, America had to resist her morally, economically, and politically. "Communism must be contained; but the strategy of containment cannot be primarily military." [127] The only way to avoid a full-scale war was to "resist totalitarianism in its various 'thrusts,' whether by military as in the case of Korea, or by political intrigue, as in other instances." [128] America had been too timid to accept the risk of "engagements in many parts of the world, both military and political." [129] Niebuhr corrected realists, who saw only a military struggle against the Russian nation-state, along with idealists, who saw only a political struggle against a global ideological enemy. America had to man all strategic outposts: "This is one reason why we are forced today to resist the revolutionaries in Indo-China, as we did previously in Greece, though we have no great confidence in the justice or democracy of the regimes we thus uphold." [130] Niebuhr advised Americans to brace themselves for a protracted conflict whose specific nature would change from time to time and from place to place. His analysis removed geographical limitations from America's sphere of interest. While he preferred a limited, flexible response to Communist aggression, Niebuhr did advocate a commitment to universal containment. If America did not acquire the political maturity to make discriminations in that commitment, he warned, "the possibility of avoiding an atomic war becomes very minimal." [131]

Asia's geopolitical status in Niebuhr's thinking was ambiguous. After the China crisis of 1949 he argued that Asia stood outside the pale of American interests. Culture, history, geography, and economic conditions simply did not bind America to Asia as they did tie her to Europe. Claiming that Asia's destiny lay with Communism, Niebuhr disagreed with right-wingers such as Senator Knowland and General MacArthur, who wanted to fight Communism there. "Our lack of moral authority in Asia," he wrote, "means that when we use military power there we diminish, rather than augment, our moral and political authority. Military power without a moral basis is always intolerable." [132] Whether military power might create moral authority he did not say. "Perhaps it would be better," he submitted, "to let go where our power does not suffice in order to hold where we have both responsibility and power." [133]

Niebuhr's reaction to the Korean crisis illustrated his pragmatism. Applauding America's rapid, initial victories, he believed that the fighting would soon end and demonstrate to the timid that the United States could resist Communist aggression without danger of escalation. He even inclined to place Asia on a par with Europe: "The Korean crisis has proved that Asia is as important as Europe in this struggle." [134] Granting the same disadvantages faced by America in Asia that he discerned before, he stipulated that "a great deal of moral and political imagination and courage will be required if we are to prevent Asia from sinking into Communism." [135] Niebuhr subscribed to the foreign policy announced by the Americans for Democratic Action: "We must have an integrated global policy, recognizing that Asia and Europe have become parts of a world that can no longer be artificially separated into Continental compartments. . . . We and our European allies are profoundly affected by what happens in Asia." [136] America must, the ADA statement continued, increase her military power and stand ready to employ it against aggression everywhere. The United States cannot shrink from protecting her global interests. "This means coming to grips with many problems, of which the existence of Russian Communist imperialism is one of the biggest and most important. Therefore, we must be hardheaded and realistic in our dealing with Communist imperialism." [137] Concerning the emerging Chinese threat, the ADA declared that the United States must prevent the extension of war in Asia and show China that to contend with the West would ill serve her interest.

Two months later, in December 1950, when Chinese forces began to repulse the Inchon invasion, Niebuhr suggested that American intervention was neither feasible nor proper:

> The military disaster in Korea faces our nation and the United Nations with the gravest peril of modern history. . . . The danger is that our involvement in a full scale Asiatic war will be the signal of a Russian advance in Europe. We have neither the strategic resources nor the moral authority for such a global war, particularly not if our European allies feel that we forced them into it by too precipitate action in Asia. [138]

He judged that "though military might is necessary in a sinful world, it is intolerable to plan strategy in terms of military might alone." [139] Niebuhr doubted our ability to win a general war in Asia, not the feasibility of limited engagements or America's permanent interest in Asia. He supported the French action in Indochina, admitting that France's plight dramatized the disadvantages of the West in Asia. A dilemma for American foreign policy arose from "the necessity of resisting Communism locally, without undertaking the fearful responsibility of initiating a global atomic war." [140] Niebuhr viewed South Vietnam's inability to survive after the Geneva partition as evidence of the futility of using military power to save Asia, but he did not relinquish America's abiding mission there. Rather, "we must bear these hazards to our cause in mind if we are, as a nation, to preserve a proper patience in the long struggle with communism for the loyalty of the Asians to the cause of the 'free world.' " [141]

For Niebuhr the American and Communist imperial hegemonies differed in the manner by which each power acceded to its role. While Communism represented a system of total evil bent on world domination, an innocent America diffidently and maladroitly assumed her imperial responsibilities. Thus America's faults are "not due, in the first instance, to our pride of power. . . . We are in the unusual position, in fact, of having been very reluctant to acknowledge both the power and the responsibilities which we now bear." [142] In a study of national states and imperial patterns Niebuhr maintained that "of these two nations the one tries desperately not to be an empire, while the other claims not to be, but is in fact a secular reincarnation of the classical quasi-universal empires which existed until the dawn of the modern day." [143] The United States had endeavored to avoid the exercise of power, in part because we had mistakenly regarded the United Nations as if it were a world government. Less conscious than Russia's imperialism, America's world dominion was also less ideological because its pluralistic character prevented the absolutism of a monolithic bloc. [144] American power was innocently acquired and innocently, if naively, exercised. We needed to temper our power and dominion with wisdom, but not essentially change it. [145] Anti-American sentiment, according to Niebuhr, derived less from Europeans' warranted fear of a nuclear apocalypse than from their envy of America's wealth and power. Besides, men inherently dislike decisions of hard necessity, such as European rearmament, "which can easily be made to appear to be our decisions rather than inexorable necessities forced upon us in common with our allies." [146]

The Irony of American History, published in 1952, commenced with the thesis that "the threat of atomic destruction as an instrument for the preservation of peace is a tragic element in our contemporary situation." [147] This tragedy ensued from Communism's attempt to conceal the irony of its history:

> Insofar as communism tries to cover the ironic contrast between its original dreams of justice and virtue and its present realities by more and more desperate efforts to prove its tyranny to be "democracy" and its imperialism to be the achievement of universal peace, it has already dissolved irony into pure evil. [148]

Tracing the American heritage of innocence to its Puritan and Jeffersonian origins, Niebuhr reflected that the end of expansion portended the disappearance of a uniqueness and innocence that we previously enjoyed. Since until recently America had existed in an unfallen condition, he worried about the effects of our sudden expulsion from the garden: "We lived for a century not only in the illusion but in the reality of innocency in our foreign relations." [149] Only after World War I did America abandon her splendid isolation. Perhaps if she had possessed the means of translating some of her ideals into practice, America would have lost her innocence, but in contrast to Russia's experience "there was fortunately no program to endow our elite of prospective philosopher-scientist-kings with actual political power." [150] Like Communism, America had always had a messianic spirit, but we had avoided the Marxist sin of manipulating history because we lacked a lust for power.

America finally, though, had come of age, and technology

gave her the implements of converting ideals into action. Christian realism, Niebuhr hoped, could offer an appreciation of irony, which would better prepare the American mission "to save a vast uncommitted world, particularly in Asia, which lies between ourselves and communism, from being engulfed by this noxious creed." [151] American globalism received the cachet of *reality*, and realistic messianism was not less messianic for its contrite heart and ironic sense.

When the Fellowship of Socialist Christians, which published *Christianity and Society*, changed its name in May 1948 to the Frontier Fellowship, Niebuhr explained that they did so in order to dissociate themselves from socialist dogmatism. Socialism, Niebuhr and the Frontier Fellowship maintained, was too susceptible to Marxism in its Stalinist form; this corruption, furthermore, they no longer thought an accident, but rather an inevitable result of basic Marxist illusions. The Fellowship still assented to certain Marxist social insights and held a critical attitude toward the institution of property, but the group committed itself to a less ideological approach to economic and political problems. [152] Pragmatism, far more than Christianity or socialism, informed Niebuhr's political philosophy in subsequent years. Ironically, he combined this pragmatic philosophy of politics with a doctrinaire conception of America's salvational role in the world. Out of a concern for America's global responsibilities, Niebuhr wondered whether America could successfully lead the world with such an inept business class dominant in American life. He answered affirmatively, because he did not believe business actually exercised formative control of national policy. The plutocracy "is more influential in projecting its view of America in advertising slogans than in determining political policy." [153] The liberal pragmatism of the New and Fair Deals had resolved the socioeconomic question at home, and we needed next only to duplicate that pragmatism in the conduct of foreign affairs:

We have to move from case to case and from point to point in achieving justice while preserving freedom in a technical society. . . . There is therefore the bare possibility that the unplanned improvisations of our early New Deal may gradually grow into a purposeful pragmatism in America and world politics. In that case we might make a significant spiritual contribution to the cause of democracy and not be consigned to the role of being merely the money lenders in a good cause. [154]

Pragmatism has been esteemed for many reasons, although seldom have its devotees attributed to it the making of a "spiritual contribution" to democratic society. Niebuhr's position on foreign policy during the 1950s, however, was scarcely pragmatic, if by pragmatic we understand, *inter alia*, an open-ended, empirical approach to problems. The pragmatic temperament does not always appreciate irony, but pragmatic liberalism is replete with irony and paradox.

For Niebuhr Christian realism came to mean a celebration of that utilitarian, pragmatic spirit which Tocqueville recognized as characteristic of Americans. The New Deal formula of securing justice through the equilibration of power manifested the "triumph of 'common sense' in American history." Through the New and Fair Deals the liberal movement in America had wisely abandoned dogma for experience and had achieved a tolerable harmony between justice and liberty by balancing one power against another in society, thus escaping the ideological tumult and totalitarian horrors of Europe. [155] The genius of democracy lay in contriving the greatest possible degree of stability so that competing interests and values would check and neutralize one another. "It is because democracy," said Niebuhr, "holds every public power under public scrutiny and challenges every pretension of wisdom and balances every force with a countervailing force, that some of the injustices which characterize traditional societies, and modern tyrannies, are prevented." [156]

Christian realism replaced the idea of the good society with the gratifications of the goods society; an older liberalism, which Niebuhr rejected in its individualistic form, reemerged in the pragmatic mechanism of countervailing power. The eighteenth-century "invisible hand," which automatically and mysteriously generated the common good out of private appetites, found its modern counterpart in the liberal-capitalist theory of countervailing power, and the bourgeois marketplace theory of truth and morality was given the stamp of *realism*. Liberal writers in America postulated that out of the self-interested competition among organized groups would happily and fortuitously arise the common good of the whole society. [157] Democracy seemed to Niebuhr at mid-century a providential confluence of secular and Christian sources, though he confessed that "democracy is not the sole or final criterion of the adequacy of a culture or truth of a religion." [158]

The new spirit of realism exalted the democratic "vital center." In order for democracy to function, parties must not differ greatly and a basic consensus must be shared nationally. Beyond a political economy of welfare-capitalism, what this consensus encompassed Niebuhr indicated in his dictum that "above all, there must be a reserve of loyalty to the nation—and, what may be more important, to the principles of justice and freedom—which transcends the party conflict." [159] The liberal nation-state in Niebuhr's mind embodied the closest approximation to justice and freedom. Applauding trade unionism's disavowal of "the blueprints for utopia to which the sensitive spirits of a few decades ago were so much addicted," [160] Niebuhr joined secular progressives once again, this time equating pragmatic, interest-group politics with the proximate standard of justice.

Niebuhr contributed an essay to the 1952 *Partisan Review* paean to America, criticizing "adolescent embarrassment" at American culture and emphasizing how we had pragmatically "muddled through" to a high level of social justice and peace. Our peril was nevertheless great, he feared, because history had thrust us into the reluctant leadership of an alliance against "a ruthless and intransigent foe, whose calumnies against us are so shockingly beside the point, that even the most critical and sophisticated patriot is tempted to become an uncritical one." [161] The temptation of an uncritical devotion to "our country and our culture" is a measure of the distance Christian realism had traversed. Niebuhr spoke for a generation—a generation that came to revere him, George Kennan once remarked, as "the father of us all"—of liberals come home, when he announced that the Christian faith could be expressed in terms of "political responsibilities" but could not "be identified with some neat ideological position or political program." [162] Few reasonable men will disagree with this proposition; yet, in fact, Niebuhr did identify Christian realism with an ideological position and a political program. At the same time, the ideological disenchantment of a generation of ex-radicals not only deprived them of a specifically Christian politics, but left them bereft of any rational standards with which to judge particular political responsibilities. Stressing the moral ambiguity of every human action, Christian realism made normative a political system designed to nullify moral values and principles. Democracy rested on the premise that there was no truth and provided, at optimum, for the balanced gratification of competing appetites. Consequently, the Christian responsibility in the social struggle "would not mean judging issues in terms of general principles but learning to understand the limit and ambiguity of every general principle and the taint of self-interest in every devotion to general principle." [163] Ironically, Christian realism demanded an intransigent defense of a morally neutral society.

Niebuhr often condemned the bourgeois principle that the commonweal is best served by each seeking his own advantage, but the moral neutrality of Niebuhrian democracy derives from the marketplace relativism of his essentially bourgeois liberalism. In the economic life of liberal democracy self-interest "must be allowed a certain free play for the additional reason that there is no one in society good or wise enough finally to determine how the individual's capacities had best be used for the common good, or his labor rewarded, or the possibilities of useful toil, to which he may be prompted by his own initiative, be anticipated." [164] The idea that limits exist to "human needs, desires and ambitions" Niebuhr dismissed as a Marxist illusion. [165] During the 1950s Niebuhr grew apprehensive of a cultural and spiritual vacuum in modern society, reminding readers of the Christian insight that security and happiness are not to be found in this world. Christian realism, however, tacitly sanctioned this malaise by refusing to pass rational judgment on the concrete ordering of society toward an intelligible end.

In the conduct of foreign affairs Christian realism did not permit a similar policy of restraint and autonomous pluralism. Niebuhr's defense of the great "middle way" at home and of its exportation limited the world's choices in the cold war to only two. His denouncement of American churchmen for supposing that "motives of service" could ever replace the "profit motive" and his observation that socialism was retreating across Europe implied that the inevitable course of modern history precluded alternatives to either American or Russian imperialism. [166] Niebuhr's assessment of the cold war and of "reality" itself drastically delimited the range of political possibility, or permissibility. He no longer considered it possible for Europe to steer an independent, middle course between Russia and the United States because, despite modifications, "socialism is still burdened by an excess baggage of Marxist dogma, and this baggage is frequently a hazard to the success of the free world." [167] Berlin socialists, for example, had the temerity to accuse the United States as well as Russia of imperialism. In the heat of the cold war Niebuhr repeatedly chastised dogmatists of both Left and Right for forgetting that "empiricism is a basic requirement for democratic health." [168] Yet it was a highly unempirical account of history that led Niebuhr to reduce all responsibility to irony. "Our moral perils," he proffered in *The Irony of American History,*

> are not those of conscious malice or of the explicit lust for power. They are the perils which can be understood only if we realize the ironic tendency of virtues to turn into vices when too complacently relied upon; and of power to become vexatious if the wisdom which directs it is trusted too confidently. [169]

On the eve of the Second World War T. S. Eliot wrote:

> That Liberalism may be a tendency toward something very different from itself, is a possibility in its nature. For it is something which tends to release energy rather than accumulate it, to relax, rather than to fortify. It is a movement not so much defined by its end, as by its starting point; away from, rather than towards, something definite. [170]

In this manner, Eliot thought, "liberalism can prepare the way for that which is its own negation: the artificial, mechanised or brutalised control which is the desperate remedy for its chaos." [171] The tendency described here by Eliot characterizes Christian realism.

Niebuhr's Christian realism, rooted in his neoorthodox theology stressing the fallen nature of man and the ineradicable quality of man's *amour propre,* remained constant from his earliest through his latest writing. While the premise of Christian realism remained fixed, it served in practice to justify both Niebuhr's former radical socialism and his later pragmatic liberalism and cold war nationalism. The fact that Christian realism was able to accommodate diametrically opposed political positions leads one to doubt both its theoretical and practical value. [172] Even as a Marxist, however, Niebuhr shared with pragmatists a relativistic concept of truth and value, a utilitarian resolution of the means/end problem in politics, and a utilitarian view of knowledge as a weapon for the amelioration of man's material condition, a view that in Marxist and liberal thought alike obliterates the distinction between theory and practice. Christian realism insists upon the radical corruption of all human thought and action, whereupon, this principle established, Christian realism is unable to specify the end toward which political life should be ordered. Reinhold Niebuhr leveled a mighty assault against a simplistic bourgeois optimism, as expressed by the secular naturalism of John Dewey and the moral idealism of the Protestant social gospel movement, but the irony of Christian realism arises from its fundamental affinity with the secular liberalism Niebuhr contemned. In the final issue Niebuhr's Protestant conception of the unmitigated and pervasive corruption of sin, together with its attendant deracination of reason, eventuated in a political philosophy that differed little from liberal pragmatism. [173] Niebuhr attempted to develop a modern Christian ethic, which he called "Christian pragmatism" but which, on analysis, turns out to be little more than pragmatism. [174] One difficulty with Niebuhr's pragmatic ethic stems from his Protestant adherence to the ethical absolutes of the Sermon on the Mount as the basis of a Christian ethic. Moreover, his formulation of a pragmatic Christian ethic suffers from an inadequate understanding of the nature and role of prudence in politics. Kenneth Thompson maintains that Niebuhr did appreciate the role of prudence in politics, though I find his argument unconvincing; Thompson's own notion of prudence most nearly resembles a kind of cautious self-seeking or cleverness. [175] But of prudence I shall have more to say later.

The liberal tradition influences Christian realism in the

domains of both faith and reason. Dan Rhoades suggests that "Niebuhr's prophetic insight has been restricted by his acceptance of an essentially liberal structuring of his problem." [176] Niebuhr, he claims, retained liberal Protestantism's identification of sin with selfishness and operated with an individualistic view of groups as individuals writ large. Hence Niebuhr regarded the context in which man acts as solely a balance of power. Rhoades is correct, I think, but we may pursue further the relation between ethics and politics. Joining the anti-rational nominalism and individualism of the Protestant tradition to a Hobbesian equation of politics with power, Niebuhr divests politics of any rationally ethical ground. This separation deepens because Protestant thinkers tend to identify the whole of Christian ethics with the absolute precepts of the Sermon on the Mount, while they also frequently share the modernist view of the relativity of human thought. John Bennett holds that Niebuhr did not altogether repudiate natural law, but Bennett does not show how such a theory critically shapes Niebuhr's thought. [177] Bennett maintains this, despite his detailed discussion of the religious basis of Niebuhr's social ethic. This interpretation is puzzling, for his description of Niebuhr's pragmatism gives ample evidence of Niebuhr's distance from a traditional natural-law theory. If one considers "essentialism"—the view that a human nature exists to which a moral law corresponds—to be a sufficient criterion for a natural-law theory, one could agree with Paul Ramsey that Niebuhr offered a "revised" concept of natural law. According to Ramsey, Niebuhr viewed man as a free being capable of infinite possibilities who reaches fulfillment only through mutual love of others. Thus the law of love forms the dynamic, natural moral law containing neither code nor fixed form but truly corresponding to the indeterminately free being, man. In this formulation all norms are subordinate to the absolute law of love. Ramsey readily acknowledges the discrepancy between this theory and the older concept of natural law. [178] This "revised" theory of natural law is probably what Bennett means by Niebuhr's "critical conception of natural law or a real Protestant substitute for natural law." [179]

For Niebuhr, then, a fundamental dichotomy prevails between politics and Christian ethics. Ferdinand Hermens has pointed out a strong strain of Manichaean dualism in this interpretation of Christian thought, a dualism that construes the world as such a dark and devilish place and human reason as so polluted by its situation in time and place that we are left with only a purist "ethic of intention" or a cynical "ethic of responsibility." [180] Unlike more thoroughgoing Manichaean apostles of power politics, such as Hans Morgenthau, who posit a total breach between the noumenal world of morality and the phenomenal world of amoral politics, Niebuhr as a Christian theologian at least endeavored to bridge the chasm. Nevertheless, the result has been substantially the same.

Ronald Howell writes that Niebuhr resolved the tension between the absolute ethic of the Sermon on the Mount and a relative social ethic by effectively separating morality and politics; like Niebuhr, Howell equates the Sermon on the Mount with Christian ethics and politics with power. [181] Niebuhr did so, Howell hastens to add, not because politics is immoral, but because one cannot judge politics by the impossible standard of the Sermon on the Mount or by a temporal social ethic that would necessarily be implicated in sin. Christian ethics can and does prescribe goals for politics; yet these humanly mediated goals will inevitably be immersed in sin and tainted with injustice. Because Christian morality is so transcendental and human reason is so vitiated, politics and ethics must always remain incommensurable. Since no one can objectively determine truth and justice, democracy provides the best form of government, especially as it becomes more egalitarian. One readily recalls Niebuhr's famous paradox that democracy is possible because men are sufficiently good and necessary because they are so bad.

It has been claimed that American Protestant political thinkers have failed to present a rational analysis of human nature and the proper ordering of society due to their basic fidelity to the "Protestant principle," that is, the principle of radical criticism, which asserts the inexpungeable sinfulness of man and judges all human ideas and forms to possess only relative value. [182] Luther desired to slay the whore, Reason, "which is the fountain and headspring of all mischiefs." [183] This anti-rationalism accompanied Luther's anti-institutional spirit in the religious and political realms with the effect that he made "the Christian ethic appear irrelevant to the logic of the political order." [184] Sheldon Wolin's judgment of Lutheran political theory also applies to Christian realism's pragmatic divorce of moral man and immoral society: "The Christian ethic might well be applicable at the intimate, personal level, and yet be quite irrelevant for the relationships created by a complicated political order." [185]

Protestant political theory leads toward either the perfectionism of the progressive temperament or the pragmatism of Christian realism. Niebuhr's abiding pragmatism is extolled in a recent study whose author warmly embraces Niebuhr's lifelong concern for "the social relevance of religion," religion, that is, in its "demythologized" form. [186] The Ancients understood the indissoluble connection between the good order of individual souls and the proper order of the community and believed that if the social body was hopelessly corrupt, then at least men ought still to strive for the perfection of their souls. At this historical moment not only does the conception of a well-ordered community seem to be a mere phantasm, but the fate of individual souls is sealed as well by demythologized, socially relevant religion.

4

Hans Morgenthau and the Western Political Tradition

A FEW YEARS BEFORE HIS DEATH REINHOLD NIEBUHR REMARKED, "I wouldn't say that the views of Morgenthau and myself are 'somewhat different.' We basically have common ideas with certain peripheral differences." [1] Customarily regarded as a conservative realist, Morgenthau complements the preceding figures in this study. The philosophy of realism, it has been suggested, tends to play a critical role in periods of disintegration, [2] and Morgenthau has recently expressed radical sentiments about the American crisis. [3] My intention is not to launch one more foray into the realist-idealist debate in foreign policy or to offer another analysis of the problems contained in concepts such as the balance of power or the national interest. Enough, I believe, has been profitably said about these matters. [4] I prefer instead to explore the philosophical roots of Morgenthau's political theory as a whole. Having considered the meaning of realism in both secular and religious formulations, we may examine a version of that doctrine which illustrates the convergence of these two dimensions and brings the philosophy of realism to its conclusion. By placing Morgenthau's political theory in historical perspective one can gain a clearer understanding of the terms of this political discussion.

One task of this essay will be to clarify and differentiate political traditions. The foundation of politics is ethics, and ethics raises the inescapable question of human nature. As John Courtney Murray once put it, "The real issue concerns the nature of morality itself, the determinants of moral action (whether individual or collective), the structure of the moral act, and the general style of moral argument." [5] Murray felt that much of the confusion in American political discourse stemmed from the fact that it has largely been "an intramural argument within the Protestant community"; [6] that Morgenthau is not a Protestant corroborates Murray's point. The jejune yet bewildering character of American political debate is partially the result of its restricted ambit.

In a study entitled "The Politics of Conservative Realism" George Lichtheim discredited Morgenthau for being an adherent of "the Western tradition" with its commitment to the *philosophia perennis*, "which on inspection turns out to be the conservative tradition." [7] The chief villains of this coterie include Plato, Aristotle, the Church Fathers, Aquinas, the theorists of absolutism, Hobbes, and Edmund Burke. This was an unfortunate assessment on Lichtheim's part. Not only are terms such as *liberal* or *conservative* unsuitably applied to the *philosophia perennis*, but to lump these figures together into one unified philosophical tradition is mistaken. At any rate, Lichtheim did indicate how in certain respects Morgenthau is a Hobbesian, and Lichtheim apparently thought Hobbes a representative spokesman of this Western conservative tradition. It should be recognized, however, that Morgenthau himself abets such confusion by periodically proclaiming his allegiance to what he calls the great Western tradition. [8] We shall have to discriminate between traditions, then, and ascertain to which one Morgenthau does belong. Lichtheim's malefactor Aristotle was correct, I believe: the best place to begin in all inquiries is the beginning. Accordingly, we must first direct our attention to Morgenthau's underlying theory of human nature, then to his conception of the relation between politics and ethics. Finally, we may appraise his view of society and politics in America.

Since his first major work a generation ago, *Scientific Man vs. Power Politics*, Hans Morgenthau has elaborated a unified and cogent political philosophy, but due perhaps to our American distaste for theory, or perhaps to our univocal liberal tradition, the nature of Morgenthau's theory of politics has been obscured. Though he has never explicitly treated the question of the source and validity of this proposition, Morgenthau has always held that "man is a moral being." [9] This affirmation has been constant in his thinking, and along with his criticism of scientific rationalism in *Scientific Man* Morgenthau implied his agreement with the classical and traditional Christian view of human nature: "Man is a political animal by nature; he is a scientist by chance or choice; he is a moralist because he is a man." [10] When examined more closely, however, Morgenthau's conception of human nature has little in common with either the Greek or traditional Christian view, and Reinhold Niebuhr's statement of his philosophical kinship with Morgenthau is highly revelatory.

In *Scientific Man* Morgenthau sought to demonstrate that power politics sprang from man's inherent lust for power and was, consequently, endemic to social life. Power politics could never be entirely eliminated from social relations, but in order to mitigate its more destructive effects man requires a political wisdom superior to the feeble instrument of scientific reason. I shall return later to his identification of politics with power and to his concept of political wisdom; what is pertinent at the moment is Morgenthau's view of human nature. Man's specific nature is not defined by reason as it was for Plato and Aristotle, nor certainly by reason elevated and perfected through grace as it was for Aquinas, but by his appetitive element, particularly his insatiable lust for power. Even though his reason is the abject slave of his passions and appetites, man is alleged to be a moral being. Morgenthau resists the utilitarian bifurcation of self-regarding and other-regarding action, insisting on the ethical unity of human action; yet the result for him is to render all human action intrinsically evil. In order merely to maintain his own existence man must be selfish, and if this simple, self-preserving egoism is somewhat limited in scope, his *animus dominandi*, his desire for power over others, is not. Human society is the battleground of lustful, conflicting egos, and the best choice available to man in both personal and public life is to choose the least evil course of action. This image of man is a secularized version of Luther's such as one finds in Hobbes, although Morgenthau does not share Luther's faith, which would at least make man justified at the same time as sinful:

> Hence unselfish (i.e., good) action intended or performed can never be completely good (i.e., completely unselfish); for it can never completely transcend the limitations of selfishness to which it owes its existence. "Concupiscence," said Martin Luther, "is insuperable." Even the action which approximates complete goodness, by either achieving, or just stopping short of, self-sacrifice, partakes paradoxically of evil. [11]

Morgenthau does not seem to have changed his position over the years, and his recent publication of a brief collection of essays in honor of Reinhold Niebuhr casts historical perspective on his philosophy. [12] "The Meaning of Science" was, Morgenthau tells us, originally written in the 1930s; nevertheless, it appears to reflect his current thought. In this essay he addresses himself to the modern crisis in which science (taken in the broadest sense of all systematic, theoretical knowledge) has lost its meaning because it has lost connection with any transcendent source of value.

Morgenthau states his concurrence with Plato and Aristotle that the inspiration of true science begins in wonder, but his understanding of wonder and the object of science is distinctly nonclassical. For Aristotle the act of philosophy, which commenced in a profound marvel at the world about us, was pursued for the sake of what he called free knowledge, that is, knowledge for its own sake and not any utilitarian end. Wisdom, Aristotle held, has for its object the first principles and causes of things, among which their good, their end, is one. [13] The wonder that captivated Socrates and Plato and Aristotle evoked a humble sense of reverence and mystery, and the hopeful and loving nature of their search is beautifully described in the *Symposium*, where Diotima compares the philosopher to the lover. There is nothing doubtful, fearful, violently assertive, least of all is there anything slavishly instrumental or basely manipulative about the act of philosophy. Only the spiritually bourgeois man

> accepts his environment defined as it is by the immediate needs of life, so completely and finally, that things happening cannot any longer become transparent; the great, wide, not to say deep, world which is at first sight invisible, the world of essences and universals, is not even suspected; nothing wonderful ever happens in this world, and wonder itself is unknown or lost. [14]

Moreover, the true philosophical sense of wonder is not to be confounded with a lust for sensation; yet, Josef Pieper writes, "that is what a dulled sensibility requires to provoke it to a sort of *ersatz* experience of wonder. . . . The itch for sensation, even though disguised in the mask of *Bohème*, is a sure indication of a bourgeois mind and a deadened sense of wonder." [15]

Precisely a fretful reaction in the face of the unknown and unpredictable provides the origin of science for Morgenthau, and his quest for knowledge is feverishly impelled by a Faustian desire "to possess all by merging with the universe." [16] Science in his formulation does not humbly and lovingly approach what are always the highest and best things, but strives to master and control "what is philosophically and empirically essential in a particular period of history." [17] In the modern spirit of Bacon and Descartes, who gloried in man's emancipation as the lord and master of nature, Morgenthau intends to control and master life in order to eliminate mystery altogether. Here we can perceive the deepest compulsion behind Morgenthau's view of science and thus comprehend his position in Western thought. The ultimate mystery of life is death, and for him as for Hobbes the final purpose of science is to surmount the awesome mystery of death. [18] Hobbes devised a scheme whereby the instinctually dominated bourgeoisie could combine the chief of their passions, the fear of violent death, with the utilitarian calculations of reason to escape from the barbaric state of nature into an artificial civil society based upon equal renunciation and equal fear. [19] Morgenthau renews the Hobbesian enterprise by enabling the autonomous and fearful bourgeoisie to appropriate a conception of science in which "the threat of uncontrollable chaos yields to the ordered unity of a system in which nothing is unforeseen." [20]

Morgenthau's conception of the nature of politics and of its place in the range of science is typically Hobbesian. His view of human nature and the meaning of science departs from that of the Ancients, and it must be remembered too that neither Plato nor Aristotle made politics the highest of the sciences because they did not think man the highest being in the universe. For Morgenthau, on the other hand, politics is the highest science, and it is in politics, in "man's lust for power over other men," [21] that the shock of terror arises. Politics is defined as "a universal force inherent in human nature and necessarily seeking power over other men," [22] though political life offers only one instance of a universal, all-encompassing phenomenon. A desire to dominate some object motivates all human activity, including scholarship and art; the ubiquitous will to power, therefore, not only destroys life incidentally as a means to preserving it but is in fact predicated upon annihilation. Not surprisingly, such a world prompts Morgenthau to agree with Hobbes that life is "solitary, poor, nasty, brutish, and short." [23] With the acute anxiety felt by Hobbes, Morgenthau declares that the overriding task of our time is to acquire an understanding of the source of politics in order to eliminate the threat to life by transforming the world.

By grasping the radical implications of the modern, bourgeois transformation of man and the political order, one may understand the continuum along which progressivism merges into radicalism; this insight will also illuminate Morgenthau's paradoxical radicalism. Greek and traditional Christian political theory established the true order of man in terms of the true order of the soul, the soul's proper order depending in turn on its orientation to divine wisdom. Man could be the measure of society, Eric Voegelin writes, because God is the measure of man. [24] The modern destruction of community beginning with Hobbes proceeded through the destruction of the order of the soul. The idea of the greatest good was replaced by the greatest evil, the fear of death, as the ordering principle of life, and the mob of passionate individuals could only be restrained by Leviathan. The classical and Christian tradition wherein the soul was ordered by its transcendent source was replaced in the bourgeois era by an artificial manipulation in which autonomous and appetitive individuals are controlled by an external power operating as a check on their instincts. [25] This was exactly the function rendered by "the mortal god," Leviathan, and, as I shall have further occasion to observe, the authors of

The Federalist Papers adopted this scheme in their theory of countervailing power. It is also the theory to which Morgenthau's Hobbesianism draws him.

The tradition of Hobbes has additional implications. When the essence of human nature is equated with the natural appetites and reason with a calculative inclination toward self-preservation, one is led eventually to the artificial state grounded on mutual terror and created to obviate death. We have seen how this is the case for Hobbes and Morgenthau; it remains to be noted how their common view of human nature engenders a similarly relativist and instrumental theory of science. In a splendid exegesis Leo Strauss demonstrated how Hobbes's philosophy derived from the bourgeois shift from philosophy to history arising out of the issue of the applicability of traditional norms of morality. [26] Ever since Hobbes, liberal theory has turned from philosophy to psychology as the key to the study of man, the modern notion of natural rights developing from an egalitarian and materialist concept of human nature.

Morgenthau's relativist and pragmatic conception of science has been referred to previously. When we realize that for him the essence of politics is will, the exertion of mastery and imposition of order, [27] we can expect his characterization of ideology as "the arbitrary postulation of absolutes, which are in truth relative to certain positions and interests." [28] Morgenthau's animadversions against positivistic rationalism are misplaced, for he stands in direct descent from that radical tradition, beginning with Hobbes, which proclaimed "the impotence of reason, or to put it perhaps more plainly in other words, the emancipation of passion and imagination." [29] For Morgenthau as for Hobbes, authority is not assigned to the reason but to the will; value is located in the historical process itself, and it is extracted by an exertion of the human will, to which there are no limits.

The radical implications of the usurpation of philosophy's supremacy by history and reason's primacy by the will are manifest:

> It is by doubt of the transcendent eternal order by which man's reason was assumed to be guided and hence by the conviction of the impotence of reason, that first of all the turning of philosophy to history is caused, and then the process of "historicising" philosophy itself. [30]

The way is opened to Rousseau's divinization of will and to Hegel's historicization of philosophy and, through them, to socialism. If Lichtheim did not recognize this, a shrewder student of Hobbes acknowledges his radical potential. [31] Morgenthau's conclusion to "The Meaning of Science" discloses the consummation of his historicization of philosophy. After reviewing its disintegration in the modern era, Morgenthau implores Western man not to surrender science, because not only his existence, but even the existence of the divine depends upon it!

> This task to preserve the specifically human in man's existence and, through it, the divine, makes of the scholar indeed the "supreme, genuine man" . . . . In the dialogue with the infinite, he is in this epoch the only one to realize in the mission of science also the mission of man. [32]

In Hegelian fashion Morgenthau implies that the realization of God and man are mutually dependent; the scholar, perhaps more properly the political scientist, falls heir to Hegelian gnosticism. Democracy has made Hegel's world-historical heroes all too common, and the "supreme, genuine man's" union of heroic passion and willfulness with the gnosis of the philosopher of history presents us with a figure beyond even Hegel's imagination.

Just as Morgenthau's conception of human nature diverges

from the classical view, Greek or Christian, so too does his theory of the nature and end of politics. In the classical natural-law tradition man is by nature a social and, therefore, political animal; while the community arises out of physical necessity and grows to preserve life, it exists not merely for the sake of brute life but for the good life in virtue and fellowship. [33] The exercise of dominion and the use of force supply the necessary and proper means to the end of a unity of order. Aristotle took the full development of human nature at its best as the standard of politics, but he labored under no illusion about the propensities of the many: ". . . it is of the nature of desire not to be satisfied, and most men live only for the gratification of it." [34] Proper education is needed to form the character of better men and sound laws to restrain and guide the many who will never be persuaded to control their own desires. Nevertheless, Aristotle was careful not to identify the prerequisites for community with its nature and purpose, and this is especially true with respect to power:

> Yet most men appear to think that the art of despotic government is statesmanship, and what men affirm to be unjust and inexpedient in their own case they are not ashamed of practising towards others; they demand just rule for themselves, but where other men are concerned they care nothing about it. [35]

Aristotle was referring here specifically to relations with neighboring states, but the point holds generally. Power is not the essence of politics, and there is no separation of internal and external, private and social, morality.

Whereas the modern mind regards any restraint upon the autonomous will as evil, St. Thomas argued the legitimate dominion of some over others in civil society on condition that the latter are directed to their own good or to the common good. This is so because there can be no social life at all without someone to care for the common good and because wiser and more just men have the right and duty to lead others. [36] Nor did Aquinas disparage the necessity of positive human law. Man has a natural inclination and capacity for the good, but he cultivates virtue through discipline and habituation, and only a rare man can do this by himself. "Consequently a man needs to receive this training from another, whereby to arrive at the perfection of virtue," and as for those who are not disposed to persuasion and counsel "it was necessary for such to be restrained from evil by force and fear, in order that, at least, they might desist from evildoing, and leave others in peace, and that they themselves, by being habituated in this way, might be brought to do willingly what hitherto they did from fear, and thus become virtuous." [37]

In an association of liberated, power-lusting individuals, however, politics is necessarily and utterly evil, since the exercise of power over someone else defines its whole purpose. The political act consists in using someone as a means for someone else, and, like Kant, Morgenthau sees this as the essence of immorality. At the very least, he says, we must always sacrifice one moral good for another, although the ubiquity of man's insatiable lust for power renders politics everywhere and always evil. All that remains for man is to console himself with the tragic sense, "to choose the lesser evil and to be as good as he can be in an evil world." [38]

This conception of politics sustains Morgenthau's theory of international relations, which are likewise defined as the struggle for power. [39] The struggle for power, of course, is not peculiar to international relations; these constitute only one arena of the human conflict extending back to the family itself. While he ordinarily describes the pandemic struggle for power as rooted in man's *animus dominandi*, in one of his principal works on international relations, *Politics Among Nations*, Morgenthau suggests that the struggle originates not so much in the will as in the animal appetites and desires, "those elemental bio-psychological drives by which in turn society is created." [40] What is significant here is not so much the somewhat different view of human nature implied as the way in which to the bourgeois mind everything, sex and family life as well as politics, becomes submerged in an unrestrained, polymorphous lust for domination and mastery.

Whether one supposes man to be driven by the will to power or by his other appetites and desires is less important than the fact that the superior, ordinating authority of reason in human action is displaced. The Ancients were hardly unaware of the force of the passions and appetites; still, they differentiated man from other animals by what was highest in him, reason, not what was lowest, and in the hierarchical, regulative order of the soul they appointed reason to the place of mastery. When reason, man's faculty for perceiving the truth of reality, is extirpated and every human claim represents no more than the assertion of the interest or passion of the person tendering it, there is no way to determine the truth and justice of conflicting claims. If we judge every moral principle as relative to its historical context, we are free to seize history and make whatever truth of it we will. The eclipse then of any noetic order ceases to matter because the key to political success, which marks the only criterion of goodness, lies in the will. In politics, particularly democratic politics, Morgenthau exhorts, the leader does not need knowledge of the ends to be pursued or even the means to those ends, but the "moral" will to do whatever must be done. "Theory" is useless; rather, what he calls "wisdom" becomes paramount, for "it is the political will that dominates in the true order of things." [41]

I shall return shortly to what Morgenthau takes "wisdom" to be. For the moment it would be well to note not only his identification of politics with the exertion of will and mastery, but also his implicit equation of political success with political right. The bourgeois world contains no cognizable, proper ends of human activity. Morgenthau stands outside the natural-law tradition, which makes reason, not will, the rule and measure of human action and law. Reason, St. Thomas explained, is the first principle of human action because reason directs action to its proper end, and in the political order this end is the common good. Reason, then, commands what is required for the common good:

> In order that the volition of what is commanded may have the nature of law, it needs to be in accord with some rule of reason. And in this sense is to be understood the saying that the will of the sovereign has the force of law; or otherwise the sovereign's will would savor of lawlessness rather than of law. [42]

From the time of the Greeks to our own, men of reflection and experience have understood that practical wisdom, or prudence, constitutes the chief virtue in human action. Aristotle deemed prudence so important that he believed that one could not be genuinely good without it; all the other moral virtues are realizable only insofar as they are directed by prudence. Yet, on the other hand, prudence cannot exist by itself without a previously formed good character, because it is not mere cleverness or self-seeking astuteness; rather, it is the habit of deliberating and acting rightly and, consequently, presupposes a correct understanding of and proper desire for the good to be done. No mere tactical shrewdness in seizing the appropriate means to any given end, prudence is the informed habit of choosing the due means to a good end. The prudent man is the good man who possesses a reasoned capacity to act well, a capacity that can be acquired only through much experience. According to Aristotle, practical wisdom "is a true and reasoned state of capacity to act with regard to the things that are good or bad for man." [43] St. Thomas also defined prudence as presupposing moral virtue that rectifies the appetite and consisting in a rational habit of selecting the due means to a good end:

But to that which is suitably ordained to the due end man needs to be rightly disposed by a habit in his reason, because counsel and choice, which are about means ordained to the end, are acts of the reason. Consequently an intellectual virtue is needed in the reason, to perfect the reason and make it suitably affected towards means ordained to the end; and this virtue is prudence. Consequently prudence is a virtue necessary for a good life. [44]

Prudence, then, has been aptly described by Josef Pieper as "the perfected ability to make right decisions." [45]

Now, to speak of goodness presupposes the existence of truth, which in turn presupposes objective reality. Hence, while prudence furnishes the standard of human volition and action, the standard of prudence is the objective reality of being itself. As Pieper points out, "the preeminence of prudence signifies first of all the direction of volition and action toward truth; but finally it signifies the directing of volition and action toward objective reality. The good is prudent beforehand; but that is prudent which is in keeping with reality." [46] It is imperative to remember that the good of man and the concrete fulfillment of prudence are not universally the same. The most basic purposes and moral obligations of human life remain constant, but Aquinas recognized that "the good of man changes in multifold fashion, according to the various conditions of men and the times and places, and similar factors." [47] Since the good of man can be specified only with regard to the manifold of persons and circumstances, obviously the most suitable means, excluding some actions intrinsically evil, to his end must also change. "But the means to the end, in human concerns, far from being fixed, are of manifold variety according to the variety of persons and affairs," [48] St. Thomas reminds us.

Above all, one must keep these considerations in mind upon entering the sphere of politics where prudence is, *a fortiori*, the first of all virtues. Long ago Aristotle warned that the educated man will look for the degree of certitude and exactitude appropriate to a branch of knowledge and that politics is not mathematics. In the political realm prudence has to do with the application of general principles to concrete situations, but neither the political good nor the politically prudent can be given general, abstract, and exact definition. Even so, Edmund Burke believed, "though no man can draw a stroke between the confines of day and night, yet light and darkness are upon the whole tolerably distinguishable." [49] Political geometers in Aristotle's, Burke's, and our own day have typically considered political questions in the abstract, stripped of every relation and ramification. They do not see that "Circumstances (which with some gentlemen pass for nothing) give in reality to every political principle its distinguishing colour, and discriminating effect. The circumstances are what render every civil and political scheme beneficial or noxious to mankind." [50] Although politics is a prudential science, the natural-law tradition excludes certain possibilities and propositions as a matter of principle. The natural law became somewhat attenuated in Burke's hands, but along with his predecessors he emphatically repudiated the equation of power with right. For Hans Morgenthau, who greatly admires Burke, political wisdom means little more than this. Wisdom for him consists in the appropriate adaptation of means to the end of success, that is, the exercise of power and exertion of mastery and domination.

In *Scientific Man vs. Power Politics*, after telling us that the political actor needs "rational faculties" superior to scientific reason, Morgenthau proceeds to treat rationalism as if its liberal, positivistic variety provided its only or chief meaning. Occasionally he refers to the classical tradition, but he does not suggest how we might draw upon this tradition, and in his indictment of positivism he often confuses its precepts with those of the tradition of the Ancients. His analysis, moreover, obscures his own affinity with modern liberalism.

Morgenthau outlines the basic tenets of a simplistic rationalism stemming from its axiom that man and the world are
governed by rational laws discernible to human intellect. The
first of these is an identification of the rationally right with the
ethically good; the second, a belief that the rationally right is
necessarily successful; the third, that education is conducive to
the enhancement of reason and, therefore, to good action; and
the last, that the laws of reason are universally applicable. [51] As
a result of these notions liberals create a self-righteous,
intransigent union of politics, science, and ethics. This treatment of the issue, though, makes no discrimination between
scientific rationalism and the principle of the Ancients that
there is a rational and intelligible order of reality and that the
good possesses a rational nature. Classical political philosophy
was not concerned with success, except as a secondary factor in
prudential considerations, although Morgenthau is primarily
interested in success. It also concedes rather too much to the
bourgeoisie and too little to the rest of our civilized experience
to credit them with attributing a moral purpose to education.
Finally, the classical conception of natural law allowed that the
application and specification of universal laws of reason were
mediated by custom, tradition, and local character and
circumstances. Modern liberalism's pseudo-religious spirit
arises less from its association of politics and ethics than from
the inherent gnosticism of the progressive temperament. The
inseparability of ethics and politics was a cardinal element of
the *philosophia perennis* that the modern tradition beginning
with Machiavelli and Hobbes repudiated, and only a superficial
observer will infer that liberalism has thereby become undog-
matic, whatever that may mean.

At another point Morgenthau rightly faults modern rationalism's neglect of man's spiritual and emotional dimension, its
positivistic misconception of society as analogous to physical
nature, and its naive overestimate of the adequacy of this kind

of reason, that is, scientific reason. Aristotle and St. Thomas, to take two cases, would have concurred that man is not a disembodied intellect nor the statesman a biologist. They would not have thrown up their hands with Hans Morgenthau, concluding that it is fatuous to imagine that man can understand himself and the world through reason. To reprove modern liberalism for its vain supposition that man can act according to rational dictates by reliance on reason alone is not at the same time to indict the Ancients who, after all, viewed him as a "rational animal." [52]

Morgenthau evidently reproaches only one brand of modern liberalism in this line of criticism, for there is another school, one he represents, that readily capitulates on man's reason, giving him over to the animal. The earlier discussion of Morgenthau's conception of human nature illustrated how he defines man in terms of his animal nature, his passions and appetites; we may now see what role reason serves in politics. Since reason is the slave of man's passions and interests, its resources are expended in what Morgenthau describes as a balancing, or harmonizing, function. Man's reason, argues Morgenthau, may inject a degree of harmony into conflicting irrational impulses, though it is unclear how this is possible, unless reason is to some extent separate from and superior to these blind impulses. Reason, he contends, can adjust ends and means to our irrational impulses; yet this role appears to be little different from that played by animal instinct. Furthermore, it is claimed that reason can harmonize conflicting ends, although Morgenthau does not pursue his implication of a qualitative differentiation of pleasures, which would lead him toward the classical position. And, finally, we are told that reason can effectively adjust means to ends, a function Morgenthau does not bother to distinguish from either instinct or mere cleverness. [53]

These are the superior "rational faculties" demanded by political life; to them one has only to add the tragic sense, the awareness that politics is inevitably evil and that the best *homo politicus* can do is to choose the least evil means to the end of success. Political wisdom is the art of acting successfully, albeit with an uneasy heart:

> To act successfully, that is, according to the rules of the political art, is political wisdom. To know with despair that the political act is inevitably evil, and to act nevertheless, is moral courage. To choose among several expedient actions the least evil one is moral judgment. [54]

Subsuming the rational under the prudent, Morgenthau identifies the prudent with the successful. Thus one gains a comprehension of the "eternal laws" of politics:

> To be successful and truly "rational" in social action, knowledge of a different order is needed. This is not the knowledge of simple tangible facts but of the eternal laws by which man moves in the social world. . . . The key to those laws of man is not in the facts from whose uniformity the sciences derive their laws. It is in the insight and the wisdom by which more-than-scientific man elevates his experiences into the universal laws of human nature. [55]

Morgenthau has not altered his view over the last generation. His latest book, *Science: Servant or Master?*, presents the gift of political wisdom as the ability to discern and calculate the play of appetites and power for the sake of success. What does he mean by success? Since the essence of politics is will, wisdom lies in the appropriate adaptation of means to the all-inclusive end of mastery and domination. In a world of blind and unrestrained appetites survival depends on the mastery of some "mortal god." The great gift in this world will be the "political wisdom" by which we "grasp intuitively the quality of diverse interests and power in the present and future and the impact of different actions upon them." [56] This type of wisdom informs the will that dominates in the political order.

These criteria distinguish "realists" from "utopians." [57]
Those who subscribe to the rationalism Morgenthau has
depicted he calls *utopians*, while those who grasp the superior
"rational faculties" needed for politics and clearly see human
nature for what it is are designated *realists*. He is highly critical
of a shallow, philistine American empiricism, both in the
conduct of foreign policy and in his own academic profession of
political science. [58] Morgenthau has argued for years that both
areas direly need a theoretical redirection; yet it should be
plain by now that the theory he would restore is not rooted in
the classical tradition. A modern himself, Morgenthau has
perhaps underestimated the responsibility of bourgeois theory
for the contemporary positivism he finds so barren and
stultifying. While advocating the primacy of theory, he
nevertheless perpetuates the modern divorce of politics,
philosophy, and ethics. Morgenthau reveals his modernity in
his suggestions for a political theory, a theory premised on the
bourgeois view of human nature: that all men are really like the
bourgeoisie themselves, that is, that they are driven by their
passions and appetites, recognizing no intelligible order of
reality with proper ends and objective values. [59] This is what
Marx meant in explaining how the bourgeoisie demystified the
world. Marx understood how the bourgeoisie mercilessly strip
away all sentimental and romantic "illusions" before the reality
of naked self-interest, how they "rationalize" the world and
show man he is master of his destiny, how at last they stop at
nothing short of universalizing themselves. "In one word,"
wrote Marx, this class "creates a world after its own image." [60]
A century later we know only too well where the bourgeoisie
and their Marxist heirs have taken us.

Readers will be puzzled when they attempt to discern the
relation of ethics to politics in Morgenthau's thinking. Morgenthau repeatedly stresses the moral ambiguity of life,

acknowledging man as a creature with a moral purpose, but cautioning as well that he is an animal who must be restrained by power. [61] As he delineates more precisely the role of morality in society, its meaning begins to emerge. He contends that morals enforce obedience to the legal order upon rulers and ruled alike and that, above all, "the moral order gives the law the standards on the basis of which the law itself, as well as its agents and its subjects, can distinguish between right and wrong." [62] While morality appears to have a normative function, whence exactly it is derived and what its nature is become clearer if we turn to the international sphere. Just as Plato held that the polis was man writ large, for Morgenthau international politics is human nature in macrocosm, though the premises and conclusions of the two men are rather different. On the international plane, Morgenthau maintains, morality plays the negative role of limiting the ends that power may seek and the means it may employ in addition to approving certain ends and means. In fact, however, morality is a product of the interests and power it serves and provides ideological rationalization for them:

> This ideological function, which morality performs on the domestic scene together with the other two, has become its main function for international politics. . . . It is not so much morality which limits individual interests, as it is the individual interests which identify themselves with morality. [63]

This identity of interest and morality, he says curiously, presents the main threat and challenge to political theory. Indeed, he might say that it vitiates the entire undertaking.

Over the years Morgenthau has dissented from the prevailing philosophy of positivism in international relations theory, upholding the primacy of what he terms the normative sphere:

> The guiding influence, however, as to the ideals, ends, and interests to be pursued by the norms under which a given society

lives, emanates from the ethical sphere. From it law and mores receive the fundamental distinctions between the good and the bad,
the ends to be advanced and the ends to be opposed, the interests to
be protected and the interests to be repudiated.[64]

Morgenthau does not conceive of ethics in the natural-law
tradition, viewing ethical norms instead as the products of
competing material forces and interests. His "scientific" or
"realist" theory of international law treats legal rules not
merely in their bare, juridical formulation, but attends to the
psychological, social, political, and economic forces that shape
these rules: "In other words, their scientific goal is to formulate
uniform functional relationships between those forces and the
legal rules. Hence 'realist' jurisprudence is, in truth, 'functional' jurisprudence."[65]

In his functional theory of law the validity of legal and moral
rules rests upon their sanction, law itself being determined by
the balance of power. If different rules, that is to say, interests,
conflict, the relative strength of competing social forces behind
their respective sanctions decides the outcome. Western
civilization has not been able to eliminate the struggle for
power, but its distinction lies in mitigating conflict through the
substitution of civilized competition for physical brutality.[66]
Morgenthau actually proposes a pragmatic conception of
morality, and, despite his frequent disavowals, he does equate
might with right. His philosophical tradition indeed has
ancient roots; those roots, however, are to be found not in Plato
or Aristotle, but in Thrasymachos's famous declaration, "the
just is nothing else than the advantage of the stronger."[67] It
should be remembered that in Plato's and Aristotle's day
sophistic moral deterioration marked the last desperate hours
of a dying Athenian empire. Realistic men understand, the
Athenians bluntly advised the Melians, that in politics "justice
is then only agreed on when the necessity is equal; whereas they

that have odds of power exact as much as they can, and the weak yield to such conditions as they can get." [68]

Thrasymachos and Thucydides' Athenians were not reputed for an excessive concern about the rights and dignity of persons, but the modern philosophy of pragmatism has a way of masking a rather mean conception of human nature and life behind a purported affirmation of the rights of man. Justice Holmes, for example, held a Boston Brahmin distaste for the bestial masses, yet was willing to allow the people to legislate themselves to hell. Morgenthau grants his Holmesian pragmatism when he affirms that the best guarantee of the freedom and sanctity of persons is afforded by a philosophical relativism that sees truth as the product of a vigorous marketplace competition. [69] A pragmatist, of course, encounters a difficult problem if, like Morgenthau, he admits that this distinctive philosophy of liberalism and its accompanying institutions are themselves relative to the historical situation of the bourgeoisie. [70] Why, then, we should accept this historically conditioned philosophy rather than any other is problematical, particularly if we claim to make an objective moral judgment. When confronted with the phenomenon of Nazism, however, Morgenthau is prepared to believe "the law of nations as well as Western civilization as a whole owe their existence" [71] to that tradition deriving from Plato and Aristotle which posits an objective truth and morality.

Morgenthau cannot finally bridge the chasm between ethics and politics. His political philosophy departs radically from that of the classical tradition, and he unequivocally asserts the irreconcilability of Christian ethics with the way men must and actually do live. [72] In the last analysis Morgenthau adheres to the Niebuhrian dichotomy between moral man and immoral society, a dichotomy based upon a Lutheran concept of morality and politics:

No compromise is possible between the great commandment of
Christian ethics, "Love thy neighbor as thyself," and the great
commandment of politics, "Use thy neighbor as a means to the ends
of thy power." It is a priori impossible for political man to be at the
same time a good politician—complying with the rules of political
conduct—and to be a good Christian—complying with the demands
of Christian ethics. In the measure that he tries to be the one he
must cease to be the other. [73]

On these terms no connection between ethics and politics is
possible. Morgenthau's combination of a Lutheran conception
of morality with his Hobbesian view of politics creates the
intractable dilemma of power politics, leading him to the sad
but simple conclusion, "we must make the best of them." [74]

As a result, moral man in politics will content himself with a
prudential calculation of the probable, least evil consequences
of political action. Morgenthau evinces little sympathy for the
natural-law tradition in Christian ethics, stating the obvious
point that it can provide only general principles of right action,
while prudence must decide upon concrete applications and
alternatives. Nor does he offer a very penetrating appraisal,
when he charges that in the past natural-law theory has been
either too vague to be meaningful or too specific, so that it has
served as a mere ideological rationalization of certain interests.
With this spirit he greeted Walter Lippmann's *The Public
Philosophy*, concluding in pragmatic, American fashion that in
politics, at any rate, it is action and not theory that counts. [75]
The foregoing must be kept in mind when one comes upon
occasional statements by Morgenthau about the existence of a
body of perennial, objective moral and political truths, the
existence of an intelligible and perduring human nature, and
even the indissoluble union between politics and ethics. [76]
These assertions not only contradict what he says elsewhere,
but insofar as he does adhere to certain political axioms and a

theory of man, they are decidedly not those of the *philosophia perennis*.

Some light is shed upon Morgenthau's political philosophy and the terms of political discussion in America generally by a symposium once held in honor of Reinhold Niebuhr. Hailing Niebuhr as "the greatest living political philosopher of America, perhaps the only creative political philosopher since Calhoun," [77] Morgenthau went on to confirm the fundamental agreement between them. He conceded that he and Niebuhr proceeded from the same Lutheran concept of ethics and politics and wound up with a simple pragmatism. Possibly a bit chagrined by Morgenthau's paean to his pragmatism, Niebuhr suggested that his realism might yield too much to Christian perfectionism, that indeed the Sermon on the Mount does not comprise the whole of Christian ethics. Niebuhr, all the same, candidly admitted to being a pragmatist who "tries to be guided in pragmatic judgments by the general principles of justice as they have developed in Western culture," [78] though he did not think political philosophy had much practical value. Reading this symposium, one cannot help being struck by the basically Protestant terms of political discourse in America, the casual American association of all that is worthwhile in Western civilization with pragmatism, and the common conclusion that, after all, ethics and philosophy have not much to do with politics.

The student of history will realize that this conclusion was the one offered by the famous realist of an earlier day who also taught that morality was quite irrelevant to politics because man was so bestial. A prudent political actor, Machiavelli warned, will learn how to do evil in order to be successful and survive. Machiavelli saw the essence of politics as the exercise of power and, therefore, as inevitably evil; prudence was the astute calculation on the part of the "lion" or the "fox" as to the least wicked but sufficiently effective means to the end of power. Somehow there is something halfway redeeming about the open and unalloyed profession of evil, something refreshing about that Renaissance counselor of princes who did not trouble himself or his reader about the Sermon on the Mount, but who forthrightly declared,

> How we live is so far removed from how we ought to live, that he who abandons what is done for what ought to be done, will rather learn to bring about his own ruin than his preservation. A man who wishes to make a profession of goodness in everything must necessarily come to grief among so many who are not good. Therefore it is necessary for a prince, who wishes to maintain himself, to learn how not to be good, and to use this knowledge and not use it, according to the necessity of the case. [79]

Machiavelli, like the Athenians of Thucydides' history, stood at a moment of disintegration in Western experience, and his advice to the Medici, like the frank admonition of those Athenian emissaries to the Melians, was advice on how to survive. Neither Machiavelli nor the Athenians were concerned with doing good in the world by making it over in the image of the transcendent ideals of equality and freedom. Thus, when a realist doctrine of power politics becomes united with a mission of universal salvation and when the image into which the globe is to be transformed is one of instability and chaos, we may be certain that we have arrived at a desperate pass in history. It is my belief that, despite his censure of naive and sentimental utopianism, the political philosophy of Hans Morgenthau shares this same messianic spirit.

In a volume of a decade ago Morgenthau wrote that the contemporary crisis of America was due to the loss of a sense of national purpose, that purpose having traditionally been the achievement of equality in freedom. He viewed this loss as especially serious because the area for the realization of our purpose had always been the whole world; now we had not only lost our sense of purpose, but we were challenged by another universal creed, and the hope of mankind depended on us. [80] Morgenthau himself spoke here as an apostle of American messianism, and his discussion of national purpose underscores the fruitlessness of the so-called realist-idealist debate in foreign policy. Our purpose, as he explained it, has been threefold: to establish equality in freedom in the United States; to maintain that ideal here as an example for the world; and even, third, to extend the realm of equality in freedom abroad in order to be better able to maintain it at home. He has, as anyone acquainted with his writings on foreign policy knows, severe criticisms of the manner in which this purpose has been pursued from time to time, but Morgenthau claims that such is the fundamental meaning of America and locates its inspiration in the Founding Fathers. I am prepared to agree with him, and I am persuaded that purpose constitutes part of the modern crisis: the imposition by the bourgeoisie of their own spiritual disorder upon the world.

Morgenthau acknowledges that the American ideal has never had any substantive meaning precisely because it cannot. It cannot because it entails a perpetual deracination of man and the destruction of any form of social communion:

> The American purpose is in consequence peculiarly intangible, shapeless, and procedural. It consists not in a specific substantive ideal and achievement but in a peculiar mode of procedure, a peculiar way of thinking and acting in the social sphere, in a peculiar conception of the relations between the individual and society. [81]

At its best the American ideal is the negative one of an escape from authority; in the past this has been expressed as freedom from political control to compete for wealth and power. This ideal makes plain the self-fulfilling nature of the bourgeois theory of man. Freed from restraint in the pursuit of his appetite, man will become the asocial, power-lusting beast he is said to be. Society in this reduced condition can never have any intelligible order and proper end to it, for the process of insatiable acquisition and appropriation produces perpetual movement and change. Thus, "The American purpose seeks the maintenance and intensification of social movement for its own sake, mobility regardless of where it moves to, dynamism as an end in itself."[82] The ideal and the very existence of bourgeois society are predicated on repudiation, expansiveness, and inevitable chaos, since it is the essence of this ideal "that the chances for its realization decrease with the stabilization of society itself."[83]

Having admitted the disintegrative effect of the American purpose, Morgenthau turns as if in dismay to the "crisis" of America both at home and abroad. Briefly stated, the principal problem faced by America abroad lies in its inability to adjust to the limits reality imposes on physical force. Hence there has been an over-militarization of our foreign policy and a failure to engage successfully in peaceful competition with Russia. [84] I have not dealt with Morgenthau's theory of foreign policy, believing that an understanding of that theory is to be found in his underlying political philosophy. His reflections on American society support this supposition. Turning to the domestic sphere, Morgenthau discovers an America plagued with a hedonistic materialism and conformity, a wasteful and irrational economic system, a cultural vacuum, and a leveling egalitarianism coupled with a licentious libertarianism. Yet the very nature of the purpose has generated the crisis, and his own version of the "American purpose" precludes any other outcome to the dilemma he observes.

> Equality and freedom are indeed good in themselves in that they are proper to the nature of man and correspond to his elemental aspirations. Yet their achievement constitutes but one of the

preconditions of man's self-fulfillment. To achieve that self-fulfillment itself equality and freedom must be directed toward a
transcendent substantive goal, for the sake of which freedom and
equality are sought. It is from such a goal that equality and freedom
receive their order, their limits, and their purpose—that is, their
meaning. Thus, paradoxically enough, equality and freedom,
divorced from such a goal and sought for themselves, evolve into an
egalitarianism and libertarianism which first stunt both individual
and social development and then put into jeopardy equality and
freedom themselves. [85]

In the political order Morgenthau finds the domestic crisis
capped off by a paradoxical accentuation of majoritarian
tyranny and diminishment of popular control over government.
To a student of Plato this comes as no surprise. Plato explained
how an insatiable oligarchic greed for riches passes over into a
democratic lust for freedom, tyranny at last being bred out of
the bosom of democracy. [86] Significantly, Morgenthau sees the
paradox of democracy as caused by technological developments and by the absence of strong leadership. [87] It is characteristic of the modern mind to regard the art of government as a
matter of technical and institutional manipulation and to trust
that all will be well if we secure effective leaders. This will be
best promoted, some maintain, if we expand participation in
power and give everyone equal access to that power. Yet
expanded and equal participation in power can be an avenue to
despotism, for the equal power of the many is as oppressive as
the concentrated power of a few. An orderly freedom is
protected, among other ways, by the vigorous, independent life
of groups standing between the individual and the state. These
subordinate, intermediary associations, such as Aristotle and
Burke held, for example, include the family, an institution now
being eradicated by bourgeois society in the name of freedom
and equality. Above all, though, true liberty and good government cannot exist in a condition of moral disorder. John Adams
and the Founding Fathers, statesmen of whom Morgenthau

approves, shared the naive Enlightenment notion that good government is possible without an underlying order of the soul and can in fact produce good men. [88] A contemporary of Adams who supported the American experiment and whom Morgenthau also respects thought otherwise. Edmund Burke wrote to a French critic of his:

> Men are qualified for civil liberty in exact proportion to their disposition to put moral chains upon their own appetites; in proportion as their love of justice is above their rapacity; in proportion as their soundness and sobriety of understanding is above their vanity and presumption; in proportion as they are more disposed to listen to the counsels of the wise and good, in preference to the flattery of knaves. Society cannot exist unless a controlling power upon will and appetite be placed somewhere, and the less of it there is within, the more there must be without. It is ordained in the eternal constitution of things, that men of intemperate minds cannot be free. Their passions forge their fetters. [89]

"What is to be done?" Morgenthau asks in a pregnant phrase. The answer is more of the same, more freedom and equality, nor could bourgeois society offer any other answer without ceasing to be itself. Celebrating the American pragmatic spirit, Morgenthau reiterates that our purpose has never had and cannot have any substantive meaning. The meaning of American life derives from brute action and movement per se; the American promise by nature forbids positive expression. Americans cannot and should not be told what to think, and only within minimal limits may they be instructed how to act. To strive for anything beyond this we would run the perilous risk of becoming like Russia!

> Conservative in philosophy and method, revolutionary in purpose—such has been our political tradition from the beginning of colonization. . . . The very essence of the American purpose, as

we have seen, is that it is uniform in procedure and pluralist in substance; as a national purpose, it exists only as a particular mode of procedure. Give it a uniform substance as well, in imitation of the Soviet Union, and you have destroyed its very essence, its very vitality, its very uniqueness. Thus, it is heartening to note and testifies to the innate strength of the American purpose, truly understood, that the attempts to invent a slogan which would tell us and the world what we are about in substantive terms have remained utterly futile. [90]

America, Morgenthau believes then, still has a purpose of universal significance: the establishment of equality in freedom as a model to the world for emulation. We must expand the scope of equality in freedom at home and extend it beyond the territorial limits of the United States. Toward this end he briefly sets forth what he calls a conservative philosophy, a philosophy that from our beginning has embodied the American purpose. Morgenthau states that he expressed similar ideas earlier in *Dilemmas of Politics* and *Scientific Man* and that this philosophy was proclaimed by the Founding Fathers and *The Federalist Papers*. [91] This "authentic conservatism" consists first of all in a philosophical relativism that assumes that no one can know the political truth; every competing self-interest, therefore, must have an equal chance to prevail, and the strongest interest, or combination of interests, must be allowed to carry the issue. Second, it posits the primacy of the autonomous individual and prescribes certain constitutional guarantees of his rights. Third, it endeavors constantly to remove any restraints on mobility, change, and self-assertion. Fourth, it constructs a rule of law and an overarching social system of "countervailing powers," which will pit one aggressive appetite against another, thereby neutralizing them, and it allots discrete spheres of action to competing forces. And last but not least important, in order to prevent this organized system of moral and social disorder from flying apart under the stress of its inherent chaos and centrifugalism, a strong, active central government must be restored. Since the whole world is to be made over into this pattern, it follows that on the international level we shall have to move toward the political organization of the globe. [92]

This is Morgenthau's portrait of America's "unique political legacy," a legacy requiring constant revision in the mode proper to it, "in the market place where the political battles are fought out." [93] The concept is not new, and when describing it long ago Aristotle thought it a mean conception of liberty.

> For two principles are characteristic of democracy, the government of the majority and freedom. Men think that what is just is equal; and that equality is the supremacy of the popular will; and that freedom means doing what a man likes. In such democracies every one lives as he pleases, or in the words of Euripides, "according to his fancy." [94]

What is new and profoundly perilous is the universal and pseudo-religious meaning the bourgeoisie have attached to their view of man and society and history. The Ancients were familiar with realists who claimed to "present[s] political reality as it ought to be presented and deal[s] with it as it ought to be dealt with." [95] I expect, however, that they would have been nonplussed by the futuristic American promise. They would not have understood a politics that seeks to emancipate man from the burden of the past in order to permit him autonomously to create a future golden age. It is not a disciple of Thrasymachos who asserts, "The great issues of American politics concern neither the preservation of the present nor the restoration of the past but the creation, without reference to either, of the future. American politics does not defend the past and present against the future but one kind of future against another kind of future." [96] Hans Morgenthau has for decades raised a prophetic voice against American moralism and messianic idealism, but the differences between him and his foes are negligible. Just as our Puritan ancestors attempted to liberate themselves from the fetters of church, society, and history itself in order to create a kingdom of God on earth and therewith to be a "beacon to the world," Morgenthau affirms that from the first the American purpose has been revolutionary and that we must continue to go forward, without reference to past or present, with equally revolutionary fervor.

The classical tradition to which Morgenthau occasionally professes allegiance did not share the messianic spirit of the modern, progressive-bourgeois mind. Political realism has always had its apostles, but neither these realists nor their opponents would have known quite how to regard an erstwhile realist who turns about to call for a "prophetic confrontation" between "truth" and "power" and for "revolutionary changes" of an unspecified, unknown nature.[97] What makes Morgenthau's recent position ironic is that he of all people should call for a divorce between the children of light and the children of darkness and array himself with the forces of light. His bitter disillusion with the promise of American life comes from his having experienced the loss of a delusive dream. More than any other society in history America has acted out the radical hope of liberation, and that is why it has failed. The promise can never be realized because by its nature it unleashes forces that can never be harnessed or satisfied.

The despair of lost faith is especially poignant when the initial promise in which hope is placed is a secularized and immanentized version of a spiritual reality. Recently Morgenthau expressed his desperation: "We know what we ought to do, and we want to do it, but we cannot. That is the tragedy of trying to be just."[98] The reader will recall St. Paul's famous cry in his Epistle to the Romans, but Paul had a faith, and hence the resources of hope, of another kind. In the end Morgenthau can offer no answer to the chaos and disintegration he beholds other than sorrowful resignation:

> Perhaps Mr. Justice Holmes has the last word with what he wrote to Sir Frederick Pollock about judging "the goodness or badness of laws": "I have no practical criticism except what the crowd wants." And perhaps we can do no better than Pontius Pilate, washing our hands and letting the majority decide what justice requires. [99]

Hans Morgenthau's political philosophy offers a paradigmatic statement of the dilemmas of American politics and society. It exemplifies the modern Western crisis, a crisis manifested in its most advanced stage by the American condition. Regardless of Morgenthau's much-heralded realism and traditionalism, his political philosophy is imbued with the modern, bourgeois spirit, and his late disillusion and desperation voice the inevitable disenchantment of Prospero in a brave new world that has not turned out so well as hoped for. The promise has failed because it must fail, and yet we surge on; to do otherwise we would have to cease to be ourselves. Liberated from history, social communion, and restraint of will and appetite, the bourgeois soul longs for emancipation from the very terms of human existence. Self-propelled into an autonomous and freely created future, the modern spirit strives for release from the shackles of finitude. The elemental American aspiration was lived out in the tragic life of Jay Gatsby who, like his creator, "believed in the green light, the orgiastic future that year by year recedes before us. It eluded us then, but that's no matter—tomorrow we will run faster, stretch out our arms farther. . . . And one fine morning—" [100] Desolation and death were the sole fruits of Gatsby's quest, and at this late hour perhaps the best we can hope for is that the "valley of ashes" will not spread from America to the whole of civilization.

Epilogue: Faith, Reason, and the Scientific Method

In the 1957 preface to his *Social Thought in America: The Revolt against Formalism*, Morton White declared that his book "is in no sense to be identified with the more recent revivals of religious, conservative, and obscurantist thinking which have attempted to discredit and seriously lower the reputation of liberalism and secularism in social, political, and moral affairs." [1] Religious obscurantism applied to what White took to be Reinhold Niebuhr's subversion of the liberal, secular, pragmatic tradition to which White was sympathetic. White's alarm echoed the concern of Sidney Hook, voiced a decade and a half earlier, that there was a new failure of nerve abroad in Western civilization marked by an irresponsible flight from faith in intelligence and the free market of ideas. Hook too identified Niebuhr as a perpetrator of this intellectual perfidy. Hook summoned readers to recapture the liberal, secular faith in scientific judgment established by methods of verification, not feeling. "The cure of bad science is better science, not theology," he averred, for "the chief causes of our maladjustments are to be found precisely in these areas of social life in which the rationale of scientific method has not been employed." [2] That one could unblushingly say this in the midst of a Second World War and the scientific extermination of peoples makes the most benighted fundamentalist look positively enlightened.

The secular counterattack must have found its mark, however, for Niebuhr subsequently repented his pedagogical error of labeling man's persistent and universal self-love "Original Sin" because such a theological doctrine was "anathema to modern culture," [3] though he still believed it an empirically verifiable doctrine. Yet there is no reason to doubt Niebuhr's reassurance that he had always intended to render his "realist conception of human nature" a servant of progressivism rather than conservatism. The secular, liberal men of good faith were quite mistaken in ever suspecting otherwise. Niebuhr's effective separation of ethics and politics and his countervailing power system of politics place him squarely in the pragmatic tradition. Faith and reason comfortably cohabited in the post-progressive liberalism of the Americans for Democratic Action, and White himself concedes that Niebuhr voted the right way, despite his wrong thinking. Protestant neoorthodoxy and the scientific method both terminated in the Neutral Society.

White contends that Niebuhr's doctrine amounts to little more than the recognition that man is not God and more closely resembles the serpent than the dove. This is a simplistic reduction of Niebuhr's position, and White's claim that the "general propositions of Niebuhr's theology . . . are consistent with a variety of political positions" [4] is certainly no less true of pragmatism. One need only recall the attraction of pragmatism to Fascist thinkers in this century, or one may simply consider Sidney Hook's Holmesian definition of liberal pragmatism as a belief "in the free trade of ideas—that the test of truth is the power of thought to get itself accepted in the competition of the market." [5] Then there is White's own position, of which I shall have more to say in a moment.

White may be right to object that Niebuhr did not always fairly interpret Dewey, and there is surely no reason to sever the link between different modes of knowledge that the pragmatists forged, even while the spurious claims of the social-science approach to politics must be resisted. It is irrelevant of White, however, to charge that Niebuhr's doctrine will not tell us "why Keynesian advisers are less likely to dupe us than planners of production are." [6] These concrete determinations of political policy are the work of prudence, but prudence seems to play as little part in White's thinking as in Niebuhr's. White holds that Niebuhr's view of history is deterministic and logically contradictory; finally, though, White's foremost concern is that Niebuhr's theological dogma and political principles are not congenial to a fervent liberal spirit. I would have thought that this was so much the worse for liberalism. One expects a philosopher to maintain that the purpose of political theory is to serve the truth rather than liberalism or conservatism; yet the debasement of knowledge to a practical weapon for the mastery of the world is a characteristic of the modern age shared by a wide political spectrum.

On one point I can agree with White's criticism of Niebuhr, although for different reasons. White points out that Niebuhr's political philosophy rests upon his theology, which demands a faith not shared by all good and reasonable men. Politicial principles based upon religious faith are generally meaningless to those who do not share that faith; it does not follow, however, that good and reasonable men must resort to the vagaries of the experimental method. Thus I am persuaded that the natural law provides the best ground for political discourse in a pluralist culture. White, however, will have no part of unscientific politics.

To his criticism of Niebuhr White joined a condemnation of

Essays in the Public Philosophy, published by Walter Lipp-mann in 1955. Lippmann's "public philosophy," according to White, was founded on the fallacious natural-law doctrine of self-evident moral principles going back to Aquinas and expressed by John Locke and the Declaration of Indepen-dence. Poor Locke was "a modern thinker who had not fully escaped the dark influence of the medievals," [7] and White demonstrates how Locke, as much to his credit as not, was really quite inconsistent on the problem of self-evident moral principles. But Locke's modern natural-rights theory, whatever its philosophical consistency, differed fundamentally from the classical doctrine of natural law; like White, Lippmann himself too easily assimilated his modern theory of natural rights to the Thomistic concept of natural law. Moreover, St. Thomas did not construct his theory of natural law on the doctrine of innate ideas or Platonic universals, as White suggests; [8] rather, St. Thomas attempted to derive certain self-evident moral princi-ples from the actual experience of men as living beings. White's contention, therefore, that the argument for universal mean-ings is circular may be true, but it is not pertinent to Thomas's doctrine of natural law.

It is true, as White says, that it will not do simply to assert that it is self-evident that there are self-evident moral princi-ples; instead, we must be shown that there are such principles. Since the whole question of natural law is too vast to be taken up here, I wish merely to propose that its principles are arrived at by reflection on the actual experience of men as reasoning animals, not by appeal to any "occult entities," as White has it. Further, we must put from our minds the modern doctrine of Locke, the Founding Fathers, and the Declaration. Jefferson's famous proposition—"We hold these truths to be self-evident, that all men are created equal, that they are endowed by their Creator with certain inalienable rights, that among them are life, liberty, and the pursuit of happiness"—expresses the theory of natural rights, not natural law. Finally, we must set aside the method of natural science in treating ethics. The method of any science or art must be apposite to its subject matter, and we cannot have the same degree of precision in human affairs as in physics. As St. Thomas says in the *Commentary on the Nicomachean Ethics*, "the matter of moral study is of such a nature that perfect certitude is not suitable to it . . . moral matters are variable and divergent, not having the same certitude each time." [9]

Now, according to Aquinas, just as being is the first object apprehended by the speculative intellect, giving rise to the law of contradiction as the first indemonstrable principle, so good is the first object of the practical intellect, which deals with conduct. Man's practical reason is directed toward action; therefore, the first indemonstrable principle of practical reason is founded on the nature of good—that is, the good is that which all things seek for themselves. Consequently, the primary precept of natural law asserts that good is to be done and evil avoided. The good is the object of our natural desire; evil, of aversion; the precepts of natural law follow the existential order of our natural inclination to what is good for us. [10] In the actual order of his inclinations, man simply as a being first desires to preserve his life and protect his health. Thus, reason dictates that human life is to be preserved and suicide, for example, avoided. Second, as a living being in common with other animals, man desires to promote life, to reproduce himself and bring up his offspring. Third, as an animal who reasons, man desires to know the truth and to live in society and cooperate with others. In this manner the obligations imposed by reason are based on human nature itself, and the moral law is said to be natural and rational. [11]

The kind of knowledge by which we apprehend the natural law is problematical in St. Thomas's writings, but for the present let us remember that the only practical knowledge all men have with certainty is that we must do good and avoid evil. The primary precepts of the natural law (e.g., telling the truth) are unchangeable (they may be added to by divine or human law, but not subtracted from) and are always the same for all, both as to rectitude and knowledge, but this is not true of the conclusions that may be drawn from them. [12] Again, a secondary precept such as monogamy is not susceptible of universal certitude. St. Thomas appreciated how circumstances modify the virtue of all acts (e.g., one would not return a weapon to a madman or traitor), just as he was aware of historical change and cultural variety. Of historical contingency and the principles of natural law Thomas wrote: "The common principles of the natural law cannot be applied to all men in the same way because of the great variety of human affairs; and hence arises the diversity of positive laws among various people." [13] The more we descend to the specific application of general principles, the less precision we have, and Thomas offered the examples of theft among the German tribes and Greek homosexuality as illustrations of the extent to which cultural variation may make unnatural acts appear blameless. It should, therefore, be clear why the most basic precepts of natural law (e.g., one must not take what does not belong to one, or one must not unjustly take another's life) have universal applicability along with great relativity and variability. Moreover, a properly historical conception of natural law has no difficulty reconciling the admixture of imperfect and true elements.

But to return from this excursus, I believe that White is still wide of the mark when he says that even if it is proved that these separate essences or universals exist, the natural-law theorist cannot show "that the principles of political morality are either self-evident statements about men in which, as Aquinas says, 'the predicate is contained in the notion of the subject,' or logically deducible therefrom." [14] I do not know what "principles of political morality" White has in mind, but only the primary precepts of the natural law meet this requirement. The principles of politics are prudential applications of the primary and proximate precepts of the natural law, or they may be merely measures of utility. Whether this or that piece of tax legislation is better, or whether central planning, spending, or fiscal austerity is more appropriate here and now are not matters of self-evident moral principles, but of political prudence about which good and reasonable men can differ. White and others may not want to accept the doctrine of natural law on any account, but discussion would be enhanced if we could at least deal with it for what it is.

There are other difficulties with Lippmann's book than those White mentions. What primarily engaged Lippmann was the problem of the moral desiccation of the Western peoples, the rot of materialism and relativism sapping our society's fiber, the advance of the disease of Jacobinism, which has become accepted doctrine in the mass education of socially and morally deracinated individuals. He affirmed that our only hope lay in a restoration of "the public philosophy" which he saw as the very heart of Western existence. Unfortunately, Lippman creates confusion by variously describing the public philosophy as "natural law" or as "the traditions of civility." As I suggested above, what he actually seemed to mean was the seventeenth- and eighteenth-century doctrine of natural rights along with the idea of contractual, constitutional government under the rule of law. This is certainly implied by his postulation of private property as one of the first principles of "the public philosophy." It is not possible within the limits of this book to treat extensively the difference between natural law and the theory of natural rights, but a few words are in order.

In contrast to modern theories, which view natural rights as actual entities, *right* denotes a relation between men in St. Thomas's philosophy. Justice, according to Aquinas, directs man in his relations with others and denotes "a kind of equality" in the adjustment between things; the right in a work of justice is constituted by the relation between one man and another. Whereas the other virtues perfect man in relation to himself, justice consists in a relation between persons, and a right relation is the object of justice. In Thomas's words, "the 'right' or the 'just' is a work that is adjusted to another person according to some kind of equality." [15] But *right* is partly natural and partly positive. A thing can be adjusted to a man by its nature (e.g., receiving an equal amount in return for something given), and this is called *natural right*. A thing can also be adjusted between persons by agreement (public or private), and this is called *positive right*. The conditions in which men live change; therefore, what is natural to a man, what is right for him, may change. For example, a person's share in political authority or the particular mode of ownership and distribution of goods in society may vary according to circumstance and the requirements of the common good.

These considerations raise the matter of the right of nations (*jus gentium*) and the illustrative cases of slavery and property. What Aquinas meant by the right of nations and its relation to natural and civil law is not altogether clear. In the *Commentary on the Nicomachean Ethics* he wrote, "that justice is natural to which nature inclines man," but man has a twofold nature, one common to other animals and one proper to him *qua* man, "as he distinguishes the disgraceful from the honorable by reason." [16] That right is called natural which man shares with other animals (e.g., the union of male and female and education of offspring), while the right that belongs to man as a rational animal "jurists call the right of the peoples (*jus gentium*) because all people are accustomed to follow it" (e.g., that agreements are to be kept and that ambassadors are safe among the enemy). [17] Similarly, in the *Summa Theologica* Thomas states that natural right may be adjusted to another absolutely (e.g., as male and female are commensurate by nature for reproduction), or relatively with regard to effects (e.g., considered absolutely, a piece of property no more belongs to one than another, though it may belong to one man for the sake of the common good). Thus it seems that all animals possess natural right absolutely, while only rational creatures judge the effects of a thing and thereby possess a right of nations. Slavery, like property, belongs to the right of nations by convention and for the sake of the common good. No man belongs to another by natural right, rather only because it is useful for one to be ruled by a wiser man for their mutual and the common benefit. [18]

Lippman raises another problem when he deals with the balance of power as the structural principle for our pluralistic society. [19] In espousing this principle Lippman was referring mainly to the relation between Church and State; he did not think a pluralistic society necessarily had to be secular as well, and he believed a balance of power would preserve a healthy independence and concurrence between the two spheres. It is arguable, however, that secularism is the ultimate, necessary solution for political stability in a liberal-democratic society; this at any rate is how I would interpret the writers of the seventeenth and eighteenth centuries. If, as seems probable, Lippmann also meant that a balance of power is the correct political principle for liberal-democratic society, a qualification that he neglected needs to be registered. The balance of power did not possess, as Gordon Wood demonstrates in *The Creation of the American Republic, 1776–1787*, the same meaning for the Founding Fathers as it had for the English theorists from whom they borrowed it. As Wood explains, the seventeenth-century theory of mixed government was based upon the existence of distinct social orders. The Federalist achievement established a system of representation in a government whose parts were separate but homogeneous; all parts of the government were to be equal, limited spokesmen for the sovereign people who, in their corporate capacity, nevertheless had no distinct part in the government. Hence, not only was any common interest between rulers and people broken, but the connectedness of interest between individuals was shattered.

Now that we have seen these difficulties with Lippmann's "public philosophy," where does that leave us? What does White offer us instead of religious fundamentalism and philosophical obscurantism? The pragmatists of an earlier day, he says, contributed "to the advent of a more rational society,"[20] although no successor to this school has appeared. We should preserve their achievements, especially their respect for "freedom and social responsibility," White advises, but what can he mean by asserting that "they have been a force for *the good* in American intellectual life?"[21] We should "advance some of their causes and implement some of their programs,"[22] but which ones? The pragmatists did well to cast off an ossified formalism, White thinks; yet they failed to provide any constructive political program. And, White recognizes, politics does require some conception of the end toward which affairs should be directed:

> A political technology does require a program. If we are to reorganize human beliefs and behavior by means of our technology, we must know *how* to reorganize it, and at some point or other we shall have to ask *which* beliefs and *which* behavior we want to encourage.[23]

White laments the absence of "students and disciples to build this technology,"[24] although perhaps they have not appeared because pragmatism left nothing to work with. "Political technology" is only an ancillary part of politics, for political philosophy must first direct the engineers and technicians what to do. White implicitly grants this by his admission that we cannot be engineers without knowing what to build. Only after we know the kind of bridge we want can we start building it. We may modify our original plans in the light of further discoveries and snags, but there must be hypotheses to begin with which will bend to meet the facts. This is the moral of experimentalism. [25]

One might inquire how experimentalism improves upon the virtue of prudence, but without a dreaded conception of the political good for man we will never have intelligible political programs or ends. Without denying the contributions of the early pragmatists it is not too much to say now that pragmatism marks a dead end. White exhorts responsible men to abandon "empty 'theories of human nature' for the solid ground of politics"; [26] it is obvious that neither he nor anyone else, though, makes a political judgment without some concept of the nature of man and the purpose of political association. How else can White speak of "a good and humane temper"? Why should we be "honest," "courageous," "rational," and "enlightened" rather than the opposite? White tells us he wants to achieve "a good society," but what can this possibly mean without knowing what a man is and what he is for?

In the end White reveals the poverty of pragmatism by stating simply that we all in fact have our own "deep moral convictions" or "terminal beliefs"; even though we prefer to have other people share them, in practice we get along with those who do and fail to do so with those who do not share them. This is sheer intellectual evasion of the problem. By this token White cannot provide any reason for choosing one idea or principle over another or for persuading anyone else to accept another's belief, a belief, let us say, that genocide is bad. [27] No other recourse remains than to accept a definition of right by might, as White's admiring citation of Holmes on life and death confirms:

"the most fundamental of the supposed preexisting rights—the right to life—is sacrificed without a scruple not only in war, but

whenever the interest of society, that is, of the predominant power
in the community is thought to demand it. [28]

White is correct that Lippmann's is "a poorly argued version
of the doctrine of natural law"; [29] nevertheless, Lippmann did
endeavor to address the intellectual and moral disorder of our
age. A great work imperfectly accomplished is always more
noble than a pedestrian one successfully achieved. Lippmann
and others who share his respect for the Ancients will perhaps
remember Socrates' gentle admonition to the young Adeiman-
tos not to be so hard on the multitude. The common people,
Socrates assured him, are not mean and are not to be blamed for
hating the present *philodoxers*. They would change, if only they
could see a true philosopher. The trouble is that they have not
yet seen one.

Notes

Notes to Preface

1. See Jacques Maritain, *True Humanism*, trans. M. R. Adamson, 4th ed. rev. (London: Geoffrey Bles, The Centenary Press, 1946), pp. vii–ix.

2. Arthur M. Schlesinger, Jr,, "Origins of the Cold War," in *Twentieth-Century America: Recent Interpretations*, ed. Barton J. Bernstein and Allen J. Matusow (New York: Harcourt, Brace & World, Inc., 1969), p. 427.

3. See William Appleman Williams, *The Tragedy of American Diplomacy*, rev. ed. (New York: Delta Publishing Co., Inc., 1962); Gabriel Kolko, *The Politics of War: The World and United States Foreign Policy, 1943–1945* (New York: Random House, 1968); Barton J. Bernstein, "American Foreign Policy and the Origins of the Cold War," in *Politics and Policies of the Truman Administration*, ed. Barton J. Bernstein (Chicago: Quadrangle Books, 1970), pp. 15–77; Walter La Feber, *America, Russia, and the Cold War: 1945–1966* (New York: John Wiley and Sons, Inc., 1967); Lloyd C. Gardner, *Architects of Illusion: Men and Ideas in American Foreign Policy, 1941–1949* (Chicago: Quadrangle Books, 1970); Ronald Steel, *Imperialists and Other Heroes: A Chronicle of the American Empire* (New York: Random House, 1971).

4. John Lewis Gaddis, *The United States and the Origins of the Cold War: 1941–1947* (New York: Columbia University Press, 1972).

5. Robert W. Tucker, *The Radical Left and American Foreign Policy* (Baltimore, Md.: The Johns Hopkins Press, 1971), p. 151.

6. Charles S. Maier, "Revisionism and the Interpretation of Cold War Origins," *Perspectives in American History*, no. 4 (1970), pp. 313–47.

Notes to Chapter 1

1. Louis J. Halle, "George Kennan and the Common Mind," *Virginia Quarterly Review* 45 (Winter 1969): 52. In an earlier essay Halle stated that Kennan "obviously does not share the delusions of the unsophisticated about the role and significance of ideology in human affairs" and thus sees men as real human beings and not as abstract entities. See Halle, "The World of George Kennan," *New Republic*, August 7, 1961, p. 22.

2. Randolph S. Bourne, *War and the Intellectuals: Essays by Randolph S. Bourne, 1915–1919*, ed. Carl Resek (New York: Harper & Row Publishers, 1964), p. 12.

3. George F. Kennan, *Memoirs: 1925–1950* (Boston: Little, Brown and Company, 1967), p. 4.

4. Ibid., p. 8.

5. Ibid., p. 4.

6. George F. Kennan, *Memoirs: 1950–1963* (Boston: Little, Brown and Company, 1972), p. 5.

7. Kennan, *Memoirs: 1925–1950*, p. 5.

8. George F. Kennan, *From Prague after Munich: Diplomatic Papers, 1938–1940* (Princeton, N.J.: Princeton University Press, 1968), p. 103.

9. Kennan, *Memoirs: 1925–1950*, p. 16.

10. Ibid., pp. 198–99.

11. George F. Kennan, "Overdue Changes in Our Foreign Policy," *Harper's Magazine* 213 (August 1956): p. 29.

12. Ibid., p. 29.

13. See, for example, George F. Kennan, "The Nature of the Challenge," *New Republic*, August 24, 1953, pp. 9–12.

14. Kennan, *Memoirs: 1925–1950*, p. 76.

15. Kennan, *Memoirs: 1950–1963*, p. 128.

16. George F. Kennan, "Communism and Conformity," *Bulletin of the Atomic Scientists* 9 (October 1953): 297.

17. George F. Kennan, "How Stands Our Pursuit of Happiness?" *New Leader*, June 20, 1955, p. 17.

18. Kennan, *Memoirs: 1950–1963*, p. 75.

19. George F. Kennan, "Training for Statesmanship," *Atlantic Monthly* 191 (May 1953): 40–43.

20. George F. Kennan, "The Future of Our Professional Diplomacy," *Foreign Affairs* 33 (July 1955): 572.

21. Ibid., p. 568.

22. Kennan, *Memoirs: 1950–1963*, p. 274.

23. Ibid., p. 275.

24. George F. Kennan, "Foreign Policy and the Christian Conscience," *Atlantic Monthly* 203 (May 1959): 44.

25. George F. Kennan, "The Evolution of the U.S.S.R.," in *World Technology and Human Destiny*, ed. Raymond Aron (Ann Arbor, Mich.: University of Michigan Press, 1963), p. 90.

26. George F. Kennan, "The 'Third World' and the Industrial Society," in *World Technology and Human Destiny*, p. 122.

27. Kennan, "The Evolution of the U.S.S.R.," p. 79.

28. George F. Kennan, "Renaissance of Philosophy?" in *World Technology and Human Destiny*, p. 183.

29. Ibid., pp. 183–84.

30. Kennan, *Memoirs: 1950–1963*, p. 85.

31. Kennan, "Renaissance of Philosophy?" p. 184.

32. Ibid.

33. Kennan, *Memoirs: 1950–1963*, pp. 84–85.

34. Kennan, "Renaissance of Philosophy?" p. 184.

35. Ibid., pp. 194–95.

36. Kennan, *Memoirs: 1950–1963*, p. 88.

37. Kennan, *Memoirs: 1925–1950*, p. 437.

38. Ibid., pp. 483–84.

Notes to Chapter 2

1. George F. Kennan, *Memoirs: 1950–1963* (Boston: Little, Brown and Company, 1972), p. 321.

2. Ibid., p. 322.

3. Ibid., p. 13.

4. George F. Kennan, *Memoirs: 1925–1950* (Boston: Little, Brown and Company, 1967), pp. 503–31.

5. Kennan, *Memoirs: 1950–1963*, p. 90.

6. Ibid., p. 92.

7. George F. Kennan, "The Sources of Soviet Conduct," reprinted in *American Diplomacy: 1900–1950* (Chicago: University of Chicago Press, 1951), pp. 117–18.

8. Ibid., p. 120.

9. Ibid., p. 128.

10. Kennan, *Memoirs: 1925–1950*, pp. 363–64.

11. George F. Kennan, "The International Situation," *Department of State Bulletin*, September 5, 1949, p. 324.

12. Ibid., p. 323.

13. Kennan, *Memoirs: 1925–1950*, pp. 403–4.

14. Kennan, *Memoirs: 1950–1963*, p. 144.

15. See ibid., pp. 327–51.

16. Ibid., p. 141.

17. Kennan, *Memoirs: 1925–1950*, p. 365.

174   POLITICAL REALISM IN AMERICAN THOUGHT

18. George F. Kennan, "Current Problems in the Conduct of Foreign Policy," *Department of State Bulletin*, May 15, 1950, p. 751.

19. George F. Kennan, "America and the Russian Future," reprinted in *American Diplomacy: 1900–1950*, pp. 129–54.

20. George F. Kennan, "Let Peace Not Die of Neglect," *New York Times Magazine*, February 25, 1951, p. 41.

21. George F. Kennan, "Where Do You Stand on Communism?" *New York Times Magazine*, May 27, 1951, p. 55.

22. Kennan, *Memoirs: 1950–1963*, p. 172.

23. Kennan, "America and the Russian Future," pp. 125–26.

24. George F. Kennan, "Soviet-American Relations: General Principles on Which to Base Policy," *Vital Speeches of the Day*, February 15, 1953, p. 270.

25. George F. Kennan, "Overdue Changes in Our Foreign Policy," *Harper's Magazine* 213 (August 1956): 28.

26. Ibid., p. 31.

27. George F. Kennan, "Speak Truth to Power—A Reply by George Kennan," *Progressive* 19 (October 1955): 17.

28. George F. Kennan, *Realities of American Foreign Policy* (Princeton, N.J.: Princeton University Press, 1954), p. 88.

29. Robert W. Tucker, *The Radical Left and American Foreign Policy* (Baltimore, Md.: The Johns Hopkins Press, 1971), p. 109.

30. Ibid.

31. Kennan, *Memoirs: 1950–1963*, p. 184.

32. See *Realities of American Foreign Policy*, esp. chaps. 3–4; also George F. Kennan, *Russia, the Atom, and the West* (New York: Harper & Brothers, 1958), esp. chaps. 1–4, 6.

33. Kennan, *Russia, the Atom, and the West*, p. 14.

34. Ibid., p. 55.

35. Ibid., p. 30.

36. Ibid., p. 98.

37. See Walter Lippmann, *The Cold War: A Study in U. S. Foreign Policy* (New York: Harper & Brothers Publishers, 1947).

38. Kennan, *Memoirs: 1950–1963*, p. 261.

39. Ibid.

40. In addition to the works by Lippmann and Tucker cited above, the reader will find the doctrine of containment treated from a revisionist perspective in William Appleman Williams, *The Tragedy of American Diplomacy*, rev. ed. (New York: Delta Publishing Co., Inc., 1962), chaps. 6–7; and William Appleman Williams, "The Irony of Containment: A Policy Boomerangs," *Nation*, May 5, 1956, pp. 376–79.

41. Williams, "The Irony of Containment," pp. 378–79.

42. George F. Kennan, "Disengagement Revisited," *Foreign Affairs* 37 (January 1959): 194.

43. Ibid., p. 199.

44. Ibid., p. 206.

45. George F. Kennan, *On Dealing with the Communist World* (New York: Harper & Row, 1964), p. 5.

46. George F. Kennan, "Peaceful Coexistence: A Western View," *Foreign Affairs* 38 (January 1960): 178.

47. Ibid., p. 185.

48. George F. Kennan, "Philosophy and Strategy in America's Postwar Policy," a lecture delivered at the Graduate Institute of International Studies, Geneva, May 11, 1965, p. 5.

49. Ibid., p. 4.

50. The Chargé in the Soviet Union (Kennan) to the Secretary of State, *Foreign Relations of the United States: Diplomatic Papers, 1945*, vol. 5, *Europe* (Washington: U.S. Government Printing Office, 1965), p. 885.

51. Kennan, "Overdue Changes in Our Foreign Policy," p. 28.

52. George F. Kennan, "The Russian Revolution—Fifty Years After: Its Nature and Consequences," *Foreign Affairs* 46 (October 1967): 16–17.

53. Kennan, *American Diplomacy: 1900–1950*, pp. 95–96.

54. Ibid., p. 100.

55. Kennan, *Realities of American Foreign Policy*, pp. 28–29.

56. Kennan, "Speak Truth to Power," 18.

57. Ibid.

58. Kennan, *American Diplomacy: 1900–1950*, p. 103.

59. Kennan, *Realities of American Foreign Policy*, p. 36.

60. Ibid., p. 47.

61. See Kennan, *Memoirs: 1950–1963*, p. 297.

62. Ibid., p. 247.

63. Kennan, *Realities of American Foreign Policy*, pp. 48–49.

64. Ibid., p. 4.

65. George F. Kennan, *Russia and the United States* (Stamford, Conn.: The Overbrook Press, 1950), p. 17.

66. George F. Kennan, "The Soviet Will Never Recover," *Saturday Evening Post*, November 24, 1956, p. 120.

67. Ibid., p. 121.

68. Kennan, *Memoirs: 1925–1950*, pp. 212–13.

69. George F. Kennan, *Russia and the West under Lenin and Stalin* (Boston: Little, Brown and Company, 1961), pp. 239–40.

70. Ibid., p. 206.

71. Kennan, *Memoirs: 1925–1950*, pp. 256–57.

72. Kennan, *Russia and the West under Lenin and Stalin*, p. 334.

73. Ibid., p. 315.

74. See ibid., p. 347; and George F. Kennan, *Soviet Foreign Policy: 1917–1941* (Princeton, N. J.: D. Van Nostrand Co., Inc., 1960), p. 115.

75. Herbert Butterfield, *Christianity, Diplomacy and War* (London: The Epworth Press, 1953), p. 115.

76. Julien Benda, *The Treason of the Intellectuals*, trans. Richard Aldington (New York: W. W. Norton & Co., Inc., 1969), p. 124.

77. Ibid., p. 177.

Notes to Chapter 3

1. Reinhold Niebuhr, "Ten Years That Shook My World," *Christian Century*, April 26, 1939, p. 542.

2. Ibid.

3. For an excellent discussion of secular, liberal thought the reader may consult Morton White, *Social Thought in America: The Revolt against Formalism*, 2d ed. rev. (Boston: Beacon Press, 1957). Accounts of religious liberalism and the social gospel movement may be found in Henry F. May, *Protestant Churches and Industrial America* (New York: Octagon Books, 1963), and Donald B. Meyer, *The Protestant Search for Political Realism: 1919–1941* (Berkeley, Calif.: University of California Press, 1960).

4. Reinhold Niebuhr, "The Blindness of Liberalism," *Radical Religion* 1 (Autumn 1936): 4–5.

5. Reinhold Niebuhr, "The Pathos of Liberalism," *The Nation*, September 11, 1935, p. 303; see also "Stupidity or Dishonesty," *Radical Religion* 1 (Spring 1936): 6–7.

6. Reinhold Niebuhr, *Moral Man and Immoral Society: A Study in Ethics and Politics* (New York: Charles Scribner's Sons, 1934), p. xx.

7. Ibid., p. 4.

8. Ibid., p. 174.

9. Ibid., pp. 179–80.

10. Reinhold Niebuhr, "Radical Religion," *Radical Religion* 1 (Autumn 1935): 4.

11. Ibid., p. 5.

12. Reinhold Niebuhr, "Morals and Mechanism," *Radical Religion* 1 (Winter 1935): 11–12.

13. Reinhold Niebuhr, "Christian Radicalism," *Radical Religion* 2 (Winter 1936): 8.

14. Reinhold Niebuhr, *Beyond Tragedy: Essays on the Christian Interpretation of History* (New York: Charles Scribner's Sons, 1937), p. ix.

15. Reinhold Niebuhr, "Taxation and Equality," *Radical Religion* 1 (Spring 1936): 4–5; see also "The Administration and the Depression," *Radical Religion* 3 (Winter 1937): 7–8; and "Roosevelt's Merry-Go-Round," *Radical Religion* 3 (Spring 1938): 4.

16. Reinhold Niebuhr "Roosevelt and the Sharecroppers," *Radical Religion* 2 (Spring 1937): 3.

17. Ibid., p. 4.

18. Reinhold Niebuhr, "The Domestic Situation," *Radical Religion* 3 (Summer 1938): 4.

19. Reinhold Niebuhr, "A New Party?" *Radical Religion* 2 (Autumn 1937): 6–7; and "The Socialist Party and the Labor Movement," *Radical Religion* 3 (Winter 1937): 3–4.

20. Reinhold Niebuhr, "New Deal Medicine," *Radical Religion* 4 (Spring 1939): 2.

21. Reinhold Niebuhr, "Fascism, Communism, and Christianity," *Radical Religion* 1 (Winter 1935): 7.

22. Ibid., p. 8.

23. Ibid.

24. Ibid.

25. Reinhold Niebuhr, "God and Piece Work," *Radical Religion* 1 (Spring 1936): 5–6; and "Christianity and Communism: Social Justice," *The Spectator*, November 6, 1936, pp. 802–3.

26. Reinhold Niebuhr, "The Moscow Trials," *Radical Religion* 2 (Spring 1937): 2.

27. Reinhold Niebuhr, "Brief Comments," *Radical Religion* 2 (Spring 1937): 5–7.

28. Reinhold Niebuhr, "Christian Perfectionism," *Radical Religion* 2 (Summer 1937): 2.

29. Reinhold Niebuhr, "Russia and Karl Marx," *Nation*, May 7, 1938, p. 531. See also "The Russian Mystery," *Radical Religion* 2 (Autumn 1937): 4–6; and "Russia and Japan," *Radical Religion* 2 (Summer 1938): 2–3.

30. Reinhold Niebuhr, "The Hitler-Stalin Pact," *Radical Religion* 4 (Autumn 1939): 1–3. See also "Leaves from the Notebook of a War-Bound American," *Christian Century*, October 25, 1939, pp. 1298–99; November 15, 1939, pp. 1405–6; December 6, 1939, pp. 1502–3.

31. Reinhold Niebuhr, "Ideology and Pretense," *Nation*, December 9, 1939, p. 645.

32. Reinhold Niebuhr, "The International Situation," *Radical Religion* 1 (Spring 1936): 8.

33. Ibid., p. 9.

34. Reinhold Niebuhr, "The International Situation," *Radical Religion* 3 (Winter 1937): 2–3; and "Our Mad World," *Radical Religion* 3 (Spring 1938): 2–3.

35. Reinhold Niebuhr, "The International Situation," *Radical Religion* 3 (Summer 1938): 2.

36. Reinhold Niebuhr, "On the International Situation," *Radical Religion* 3 (Spring 1938):5.

37. Ibid.

38. See, for example, Reinhold Niebuhr, "After Munich," *Radical Religion* 4 (Winter 1938): 1–2; "Peace and the Liberal Illusion," *Nation*, January 28, 1939, pp. 117–19; "Some Reflections on the Retreat of Democracy," *Radical Religion* 4 (Spring 1939): 5–8.

39. See Reinhold Niebuhr, "The New Horrors of War," *Radical Religion* 2 (Autumn 1937): 4; and "The International Situation," *Radical Religion* 3 (Autumn 1938): 1–2.

40. Reinhold Niebuhr, "The International Situation," *Radical Religion* 4 (Summer 1939): 1–2; and "Tyranny and War," *Radical Religion* 4 (Autumn 1939): 8–9.

41. Reinhold Niebuhr, *Christianity and Power Politics* (New York: Charles Scribner's Sons, 1952), pp. 16–17. A thoughtful evaluation of Niebuhr's criticism of pacifism may be found in James F. Childress, "Reinhold Niebuhr's Critique of Pacifism," *Review of Politics* 36 (October 1974): 467–91.

42. Reinhold Niebuhr, "Politics and the Christian Ethic," *Christianity and Society* 5 (Spring 1940):25.

43. Ibid., p. 27.

44. Niebuhr, *Christianity and Power Politics*, p. 30.

45. See, for example, Reinhold Niebuhr, "Christianity and the World Crisis," *Christianity and Society* 5 (Fall 1940): 3–4; "Critical Loyalty," *Christianity and Crisis*, June 30, 1941, p. 2; "An Ineffectual Sermon on Love," *Christianity and Crisis*, December 15, 1941, pp. 2–3.

46. Reinhold Niebuhr, "Christian Moralism in America," *Radical Religion* 5 (Winter 1940): 17. See also "American Neutrality," *Christianity and Society* 5 (Summer 1940): 5–7; "The International Situation," *Christianity and Society* 5 (Fall 1940): 1–2; and "America in the Hour of Decision," *Christianity and Society* 6 (Summer 1941): 1–3.

47. Reinhold Niebuhr, "To Prevent the Triumph of an Intolerable Tyranny," *The Christian Century*, December 18, 1940, p. 1578.

48. Reinhold Niebuhr, "The War Situation," *Christianity and Society* 6 (Winter 1940): 4.

49. Reinhold Niebuhr, "New Allies, Old Issues," *Nation*, July 19, 1941, pp. 50–52.

50. Reinhold Niebuhr, "Russia and the West," *Nation*, January 16, 1943, pp. 82–84; also "Russia and the West," *Nation*, January 23, 1943, pp. 124–125.

51. Reinhold Niebuhr, "The Perils of Our Foreign Policy," *Christianity and Society* 8 (Spring 1943):21.

52. Reinhold Niebuhr, "Marxism in Eclipse," *Spectator*, June 4, 1943, p. 519.

53. Reinhold Niebuhr, "The Communist Party and Russia," *Christianity and Society* 9 (Spring 1944): 9; see also letter to the editor on "Russia and the Communist Party," *Nation*, April 10, 1943, p. 537.

54. Reinhold Niebuhr, "Russia and the Post-War World," *Christianity and Society* 10 (Winter 1944):5.

55. Reinhold Niebuhr, "Russia and the Peace," *Christianity and Crisis*, November 13, 1944, p. 2.

56. It is not my purpose here to examine directly Niebuhr's neoorthodox theology. This has been done elsewhere and at length. There are a number of studies of Niebuhr's theology and general social thought, including a comprehensive treatment by Gordon Harland, *The Thought of Reinhold Niebuhr* (New York: Oxford University Press, 1960). Also, a valuable collection of critical essays by distinguished scholars is to be found in Charles W. Kegley and Robert W. Bretall, eds., *Reinhold Niebuhr: His Religious, Social and Political Thought* (New York: The Macmillan Co., 1956). The point I wish to make is that the neoorthodox theology that underlies Niebuhr's whole realist ethical and political philosophy and that he elaborately sets forth in his two-volume *The Nature and Destiny of Man: A Christian Interpretation* (New York: Charles Scribner's Sons, 1947) readily accommodates both his earlier radical socialism and his later pragmatic liberalism. The realist theology does not change; its practical implications do.

57. Reinhold Niebuhr, *The Children of Light and the Children of Darkness: A Vindication of Democracy and a Critique of Its Traditional Defense* (New York: Charles Scribner's Sons, 1944), p. xi.

58. Ibid., p. 9.

59. Ibid., pp. 10–11.

60. Ibid., p. 17.

61. Reinhold Niebuhr, "Politics and Economics," *Christianity and Society* 7 (Autumn 1942): 7.

62. Ibid., p. 8.

63. Reinhold Niebuhr, "Factors of Cohesion," *Spectator*, June 18, 1943, p. 562; see also "The Pillars of Peace," *Spectator*, October 22, 1943, pp. 378–79; and "Great Britain's Post-War Role," *Nation*, July 10, 1943, pp. 39–40.

64. Reinhold Niebuhr, "The Possibility of a Durable Peace," *Christianity and Society* 8 (Summer 1943):10.

65. Reinhold Niebuhr, "Realistic Internationalism," *Christianity and Society* 9 (Fall 1944):5.

66. Reinhold Niebuhr, "From Wilson to Roosevelt," *Christianity and Society* 8 (Fall 1943): 4.

67. Reinhold Niebuhr, "Democratic Goals and World Order," *New Leader*, September 23, 1944, pp. 4–5.

68. Reinhold Niebuhr, "Nationalism and the Possibilities of Internationalism," *Christianity and Society* 8 (Fall 1943): 5.

69. Ibid, p. 6.

70. Reinhold Niebuhr, "Is This 'Peace in Our Time'?" *Nation*, April 7, 1945, p. 383.

71. Reinhold Niebuhr, "Anglo-Saxon Tensions," *Spectator*, February 16, 1945, p. 142; see also "The Conference of the 'Big Three,'" *Christianity and Crisis*, March 5, 1945, pp. 1–2.

72. Reinhold Niebuhr, "Russia and the West," *Christianity and Society* 10 (Summer 1945): 6; see also "The Russian Enigma," *Christianity and Society* 11 (Winter 1945): 4–6.

73. Reinhold Niebuhr, "Will America Back Out?" *Nation*, January 13, 1945, pp. 42–43.

74. Reinhold Niebuhr, "Editorial Notes," *Christianity and Crisis*, June 25, 1945, p. 2.

75. Reinhold Niebuhr, "The Atomic Bomb," *Christianity and Society* 10 (Fall 1945) 3–5.

76. Reinhold Niebuhr, "The Atomic Issue," *Christianity and Crisis*, October 15, 1945, p. 7.

77. Reinhold Niebuhr, "Our Relations to Japan," *Christianity and Crisis*, September 17, 1945, p. 6.

78. Reinhold Niebuhr, "The End of the War," *Christianity and Society* 10 (Fall 1945): 7.

79. See, for example, Reinhold Niebuhr, "The International Situation," *Christianity and Society* 11 (Summer 1946): 3–4; "The Russian and American Race," *Christianity and Society* 11 (Summer 1946): 6–7; "The Ideological Factors in the World Situation," *Christianity and Society* 11 (Summer 1946): 4–6; and "The Middle Way," *Christianity and Society* 12 (Winter 1946): 4–5.

80. Reinhold Niebuhr, "Positive Defense," *Christianity and Crisis*, April 29, 1946, pp. 1–2; see also "Europe, Russia, and America," *Nation*, September 14, 1946, pp. 288–89.

81. Reinhold Niebuhr, "Our Relations to Russia," in *Toward a Better World,* ed. William Scarlett (Philadelphia: John C. Winston, Co., 1946), pp. 123–32; see also "The Conflict Between Nations and Nations and Between Nations and God," *Christianity and Crisis,* August 5, 1946, pp. 2–4; and "The World Situation," *Christianity and Society* 11 (Fall 1946): 3.

82. Reinhold Niebuhr, "As Others See Us," *Christianity and Crisis,* December 9, 1946, p. 5.

83. Reinhold Niebuhr, "The Fight for Germany," *Life,* October 21, 1946, p. 72.

84. Ibid., p. 65.

85. Reinhold Niebuhr, "Mr. Wallace's Errors," *Christianity and Crisis,* October 28, 1946, p. 1.

86. Reinhold Niebuhr, "Our Chances for Peace," *Christianity and Crisis,* February 17, 1947, p. 1.

87. Ibid., p. 2.

88. Reinhold Niebuhr, "The Organization of the Liberal Movement," *Christianity and Society* 12 (Spring 1947): 8.

89. Reinhold Niebuhr, "America's Precarious Eminence," *Virginia Quarterly Review* 23 (Autumn 1947): 482.

90. Reinhold Niebuhr, "American Power and European Health," *Christianity and Crisis,* June 9, 1947, p. 1.

91. Ibid.

92. Reinhold Niebuhr, "Editorial Notes," *Christianity and Crisis,* August 4, 1947, p. 2.

93. Reinhold Niebuhr, "The Marshall Plan," *Christianity and Crisis,* October 13, 1947, p. 2; see also "American Wealth and the World's Poverty," *Christianity and Society* 12 (Autumn 1947): 3–4.

94. Reinhold Niebuhr, "Editorial Notes," *Christianity and Crisis,* February 16, 1948, p. 10.

95. See, for example, Reinhold Niebuhr, "The Federation of Western Europe," *Christianity and Crisis,* March 1, 1948, pp. 17–18; and "Amid Encircling Doom," *Christianity and Crisis,* April 12, 1948, pp. 41–42.

96. Reinhold Niebuhr, "America's Eminence," *Christianity and Society* 13 (Summer 1948): 3.

97. Ibid., p. 4.

98. Reinhold Niebuhr, "For Peace, We Must Risk War," *Life,* September 20, 1948, p. 38.

99. Ibid., p. 39.

100. Reinhold Niebuhr, "American Pride and Power," *American Scholar* 17 (Autumn 1948): 393.

101. Reinhold Niebuhr, "They All Fear America," *Christian Century,* August 20, 1947, pp. 993–94.

102. Reinhold Niebuhr, "Can We Avoid Catastrophe?" *Christian Century,* May 26, 1948, p. 505.

103. Reinhold Niebuhr, "Hazards and Resources," *Virginia Quarterly Review* 25 (Spring 1949): 203.

104. Ibid., p. 204.

105. Reinhold Niebuhr, "Revision of the United Nations Charter," *Christianity and Society* 13 (Summer 1948): 8.

106. Reinhold Niebuhr, "The Illusion of World Government," *Foreign Affairs* 27 (April 1949): 379.

107. Ibid., p. 382.

108. Ibid., p. 388.

109. Reinhold Niebuhr, "The Moral Implications of Loyalty to the United Nations," *Hazen Pamphlets*, no. 29 (New Haven, Conn.: Edward W. Hazen Foundation, Inc., 1952), p. 7.

110. Ibid., pp. 7–8.

111. Ibid., p. 11.

112. Reinhold Niebuhr, "The Quaker Way," *Christianity and Society* 15 (Winter 1949–50): 4–6.

113. Reinhold Niebuhr, "The North Atlantic Pact," *Christianity and Crisis*, May 30, 1949, p. 65.

114. Ibid.

115. Ibid., p. 66.

116. Ibid.

117. See, for example, Reinhold Niebuhr, "Editorial Notes," *Christianity and Crisis*, February 6, 1950, p. 2; and "Editorial Notes," *Christianity and Crisis*, February 20, 1950, pp. 10–11.

118. Reinhold Niebuhr, "The Hydrogen Bomb," *Christianity and Society* 15 (Spring 1950): 5.

119. Reinhold Niebuhr, "Co-Existence or Total War," *Christian Century*, August 18, 1954, p. 972; see also "The Conditions of Our Survival," *Virginia Quarterly Review* 26 (Autumn 1950): 481–91; and "Alternatives to the H-Bomb," *New Leader*, August 2, 1954, pp. 12–14.

120. Niebuhr, "Co-Existence or Total War," p. 972.

121. Reinhold Niebuhr, "Religious Politics," *Christianity and Society* 16 (Autumn 1951): 4.

122. Reinhold Niebuhr, *Christian Realism and Political Problems* (New York: Charles Scribner's Sons, 1953), p. 119.

123. Ibid., p. 120.

124. Reinhold Niebuhr, "A Protest against a Dilemma's Two Horns," *World Politics* 2 (April 1950): 341.

125. See Reinhold Niebuhr, "The Mastery of History," *Christianity and Society* 16 (Spring 1951): 6–7; and "The Evil of the Communist Idea," *New Leader*, June 8, 1953, pp. 16–18.

126. See Reinhold Niebuhr, "The Peril of Complacency in our Nation," *Christianity and Crisis*, February 8, 1954, 1–2.

127. Niebuhr, "A Protest against a Dilemma's Two Horns," p. 344.

128. Reinhold Niebuhr, "The World Council and the Peace Issue," *Christianity and Crisis*, August 7, 1950, p. 107.

129. Ibid.

130. Reinhold Niebuhr, "The Two Dimensions of the Struggle," *Christianity and Crisis*, May 28, 1951, p. 65.

131. Ibid., p. 66. See also Reinhold Niebuhr, "The Peril of War and the Prospects of Peace," *Christianity and Crisis*, October 15, 1951, pp. 129–30.

132. Reinhold Niebuhr, "American Conservatism and the World Crisis: A Study in Vacillation," *Yale Review* 40 (March 1951): 394–95. See also "Communism and Christianity in Asia," *Christianity and Society* 14 (Summer 1949): 7–8; "Communism in China," *Christianity and Society* 15 (Winter 1949–50): 6–7; "The Anatomy of American Nationalism," *New Leader*, February 28, 1955, pp. 16–17.

133. Reinhold Niebuhr, "Hybris," *Christianity and Society* 16 (Spring 1951): 6.

134. Reinhold Niebuhr, "Editorial Notes," *Christianity and Crisis*, October 16, 1950, p. 130.

135. Ibid.

136. Americans for Democratic Action, "A United States Policy for Asia: A Policy Statement," *Christianity and Crisis*, October 16, 1950, p. 133.

137. Ibid., p. 134.

138. Reinhold Niebuhr, "Editorial Notes," *Christianity and Crisis*, December 25, 1950, p. 170.

139. Ibid.

140. Reinhold Niebuhr, "America and the Asians," *New Leader*, May 31, 1954, p. 4.

141. Reinhold Niebuhr, "The Developments in Indo-China," *Christianity and Society* 19 (special issue, 1954): 4.

142. Reinhold Niebuhr, *The Self and the Dramas of History* (New York: Charles Scribner's Sons, 1955), p. 211.

143. Reinhold Niebuhr, *The Structure of Nations and Empires* (New York: Charles Scribner's Sons, 1959), p. 9.

144. Ibid., p. 10.

145. See Reinhold Niebuhr, "The American Power," *Christianity and Society* 16 (Autumn 1951): 6–8.

146. Reinhold Niebuhr, "Why They Dislike America," *New Leader*, April 12, 1954, p. 4.

147. Reinhold Niebuhr, *The Irony of American History* (New York: Charles Scribner's Sons, 1952), p. vii.

148. Ibid., p. viii.

149. Ibid., p. 35.

150. Ibid., pp. 3–4.

151. Ibid., p. 16.

152. See Reinhold Niebuhr, "Frontier Fellowship," *Christianity and Society* 13 (Autumn 1948): 3; and "The Second Focus of the Fellowship," *Christianity and Society* 15 (Winter 1949–50): 19–22.

153. Reinhold Niebuhr, "Plutocracy and World Responsibilities," *Christianity and Society* 14 (Autumn 1949): 7.

154. Ibid., p. 8.

155. Niebuhr, *The Irony of American History*, pp. 89–108; and *The Self and the Dramas of History*, pp. 200–201. See also Reinhold Niebuhr, "Halfway to What?" *Nation*, January 14, 1950, pp. 26–28; "We Need an Edmund Burke," *Christianity and Society* 16 (Summer 1951): 6–8; and "Coercion, Self-Interest, and Love," in *The Organizational Revolution: A Study in the Ethics of Economic Organization*, ed. Kenneth E. Boulding (New York: Harper & Brothers, 1953), pp. 228–44.

156. Reinhold Niebuhr, "Democracy, Secularism, and Christianity," *Christianity and Crisis*, March 2, 1953, p. 20.

157. The limits of the present study prevent me from offering an extended discussion of liberal pluralist theory. The literature pertaining to this subject is sizable; for a start, the interested reader will find several seminal statements of this theory in the following works: John Kenneth Galbraith, *American Capitalism: The Concept of Countervailing Power*, 2d ed. rev. (Boston: Houghton Mifflin Co., 1956); Arthur M. Schlesinger, Jr., *The Vital Center: The Politics of Freedom* (Boston: Houghton Mifflin Co., 1949); Daniel Bell, *The End of Ideology: On the Exhaustion of Political Ideas in the Fifties*, rev. ed. (New York: The Free Press, 1962); Seymour Martin Lipset, *Political Man: The Social Bases of Politics* (New York: Doubleday & Co., Inc., 1960).

158. Niebuhr, "Democracy, Secularism, and Christianity," p. 24.

159. Reinhold Niebuhr, "Democracy and the Party Spirit," *New Leader*, March 15, 1954, p. 4.

160. Reinhold Niebuhr, "The Meaning of Labor Unity," *New Leader*, March 28, 1955, p. 9; and "The CIO-AFL Merger and the Labor Movement," *Christianity and Society* 20 (Spring 1955): 5–6.

161. Reinhold Niebuhr, "Our Country and Our Culture: A Symposium," *Partisan Review* 19 (May–June 1952): 302.

162. Reinhold Niebuhr, "Our Faith and Concrete Political Decisions," *Christianity and Society* 17 (Summer 1952): 3.

163. Reinhold Niebuhr, "Christian Faith and Social Action," in *Christian Faith and Social Action*, ed. John A. Hutchinson (New York: Charles Scribner's Sons, 1953), p. 238.

164. Reinhold Niebuhr, "The Christian Faith and the Economic Life of Liberal Society," in *Goals of Economic Life*, ed. A. Dudley Ward (New York: Harper & Brothers, 1953), p. 446.

165. Quoted in John C. Bennett, "Reinhold Niebuhr's Social Ethics," in *Reinhold Niebuhr: His Religious, Social and Political Thought*, p. 74.

166. See Reinhold Niebuhr, "Communism and the Clergy," *Christian Century*, August 19, 1953, pp. 936–37; and "The Fate of European Socialism," *New Leader*, June 20, 1955, pp. 6–8.

167. Reinhold Niebuhr, "The Anomaly of European Socialism," *Yale Review* 42 (December 1952): 161.

168. Ibid., p. 166.

169. Niebuhr, *The Irony of American History*, p. 133.

170. T. S. Eliot, *Christianity and Culture: The Idea of a Christian Society and Notes Towards the Definition of Culture* (New York: Harcourt, Brace & World, Inc., 1949), p. 12.

171. Ibid.

172. Kenneth Thompson, taking a different viewpoint from mine, has also cited realism's lack of explanatory power; see "The Political Philosophy of Reinhold Niebuhr," in *Reinhold Niebuhr: His Religious, Social and Political Thought*, pp. 152–75.

173. See Wilson Carey McWilliams, "Reinhold Niebuhr: New Orthodoxy for an Old Liberalism," *American Political Science Review* 56 (December 1962): 874–85. McWilliams maintains, as I have, that "Niebuhr's basic political ideas are essentially the same as those of the liberals he seeks to criticize" (p. 874). Specifically, he argues that Niebuhr holds the liberal doctrines of human perfectibility, the evaluation of freedom as the *summum bonum* of society, the contract theory of the state, and the idea of historical progress. While it is an astute and cogent analysis, I have some reservations about it, particularly McWilliams's suggestion that Niebuhr's "theory contains an implicit 'natural law' or 'natural right' " (p. 877), which, of course, are not the same thing, and his belief that "for Niebuhr the free man is in essence the good man; virtue follows automatically from freedom. Man's imperfections arise from his involvement in nature—an inevitable involvement, to be sure, but one rooted in lack of power and not of virtue in the classical sense" (p. 885). Quite the contrary, the free man is not the good man in Niebuhr's Lutheran conception of human nature and sin. McWilliams misinterprets, I think, Niebuhr's realism as a rational doctrine concerning man's situation in physical nature, thereby ignoring the theological heart of Christian realism. It is the centrality of sin in Niebuhr's neoorthodox theology that allows the conjunction of Christian realism and secular liberalism and their common commitment to a contentless freedom as the prerequisite for the exertion of mastery in the world and the enlightened pursuit of individual will and appetite. This is perhaps, among other things, the bond felt by those Morton White calls "atheists for Niebuhr." It may be replied that Niebuhr makes love the ultimate ethical norm, but I am persuaded that his use of this norm is either practically irrelevant or only compounds man's sinfulness in a sinful world. John Bennett's essay "Reinhold Niebuhr's Social Ethics" admits the tenuous connection between love and social ethics in Niebuhr's thought, although Bennett contends that it does exist.

174. See Reinhold Niebuhr, "The Problem of a Protestant Social Ethic," *Union Seminary Quarterly Review* 15 (November 1959): 1–11.

175. See Kenneth W. Thompson, "Beyond National Interest: A Critical Evaluation of Reinhold Niebuhr's Theory of International Politics," *Review of Politics* 17 (April 1955): 167–88; and "The Political Philosophy of Reinhold Niebuhr." Thompson prefers not to deal with politics in even proximate moral terms; instead, moral principles should be derived from political practice. Self-interest, according to Thompson, can be overcome only by enlarging the scope of mutual interests.

176. Dan Rhoades, "The Prophetic Insight and Theoretical-Analytical Inadequacy of 'Christian Realism,' " *Ethics* 75 (October 1964): 1. The substance and language of Rhoades's discussion reveal his predilection for the social science approach to politics. He believes that neither individualism, which he erroneously equates with any political theory based on a conception of human nature, nor a sound doctrine of sin can give us concrete political answers. That neither is intended to do so, at least immediately, does

not occur to Rhoades; the absence of any understanding of prudence among moderns is remarkable. For Rhoades, then, we would do better to follow the example of the social sciences, which take man as an actor "within various structural fields" and pay more attention to methodology and empirical analysis. On the modernist perversion of science through an absorption in methodology, see Eric Voegelin, *The New Science of Politics* (Chicago: University of Chicago Press, 1952). A fuller treatment of Niebuhr's relation to liberal Protestant theology may be found in Edward D. O'Connor, C.S.C., "The Theology of Reinhold Niebuhr," *Review of Politics* 23 (April 1961): 172–202.

177. Bennett, "Reinhold Niebuhr's Social Ethics," p. 56.

178. Paul Ramsey, "Love and Law," in *Reinhold Niebuhr: His Religious, Social and Political Thought*, pp. 80–123.

179. Bennett, "Reinhold Niebuhr's Social Ethics," p. 56.

180. Ferdinand A. Hermens, "Ethics, Politics, and Power: Christian Realism and Manichaean Dualism," *Ethics* 68 (July 1958): 246–59.

181. Ronald F. Howell, "Political Philosophy on a Theological Foundation: An Expository Analysis of the Political Thought of Reinhold Niebuhr," *Ethics* 63 (January 1953): 79–99.

182. Douglas Sturm, "A Critique of American Protestant Social and Political Thought," *Journal of Politics* 26 (November 1964): 896–913.

183. Martin Luther, *A Commentary on St. Paul's Epistle to the Galatians* in *Martin Luther: Selections from His Writings*, ed. John Dillenberger (New York: Anchor Books, 1961), p. 128.

184. Sheldon S. Wolin, "Politics and Religion: Luther's Simplistic Imperative," *American Political Science Review* 50 (March 1956): 40.

185. Ibid., p. 41.

186. See Ronald Stone, *Reinhold Niebuhr: Prophet to Politicians* (Nashville, Tenn.: Abingdon Press, 1972). Another favorable appraisal of Niebuhr's "pragmatism in a theological context" is contained in Roger L. Shinn, "Realism, Radicalism, and Eschatology in Reinhold Niebuhr: A Reassessment" in *The Legacy of Reinhold Niebuhr*, ed. Nathan A. Scott, Jr., (Chicago: University of Chicago Press, 1975), pp. 85–99. In the same volume Franklin Gamwell argues that Niebuhr was no secularist and that his contribution to political theory was to show the "relevance" of a theistic ethic to political problems. Gamwell thinks Niebuhr's effort had its shortcomings, but one of them was not a pragmatic concern for divine utility.

Notes to Chapter 4

1. Reinhold Niebuhr and Hans Morgenthau, "The Ethics of War and Peace in the Nuclear Age," *War/Peace Report* 7 (February 1967): 3.

2. See John S. Dunne, C.S.C., "Realpolitik in the Decline of the West," *Review of Politics* 21 (January 1959): 131–50.

3. Hans J. Morgenthau, *Truth and Power: Essays of a Decade, 1960–70* (New York: Praeger, 1970).

4. A few of the abler analyses of this sort are George R. Geiger, "Retreat to What?" *Antioch Review* 6 (December 1946): 625–27; Arnold Wolfers, "Statesmanship and Moral Choice," *World Politics* 1 (January 1949): 175–95; Myres S. McDougal, "Law and Power," *American Journal of International Law* 46 (January 1952): 102–14; Robert W. Tucker, "Professor Morgenthau's Theory of Political 'Realism,' " *American Political Science Review* 46 (March 1952): 214–24; Frank Tannenbaum, "The Balance of Power Versus the Coordinate State," *Political Science Quarterly* 67 (June 1952): 173–97; Warner R. Schilling, "The Clarification of Ends Or, Which Interest Is the National?", *World Politics* 8 (July 1956); 566–78; Stanley H. Hoffmann, "International Relations: The Long Road to Theory," *World Politics* 11 (April 1959): 346–77; Robert W. Tucker, "Political Realism and Foreign Policy," *World Politics* 13 (April 1961): 461–70; and Inis L. Claude, Jr., *Power and International Relations* (New York: Random House, 1962). A book that brings the social science approach to the realist-idealist debate is John H. Herz, *Political Realism and Political Idealism* (Chicago: University of Chicago Press, 1951). In addition to Herz's book the reader will find similar syntheses of realistic idealism in Donald Brandon, *American Foreign Policy: Beyond Utopianism and Realism* (New York: Appleton-Century-Crofts, 1966), and Thomas I. Cook and Malcolm Moos, "Foreign Policy: The Realism of Idealism," *American Political Science Review* 46 (June 1952): 343–56.

5. John Courtney Murray, S.J., *We Hold These Truths: Catholic Reflections on the American Proposition* (New York: Sheed and Ward, 1960), p. 282.

6. Ibid., p. 285.

7. George Lichtheim, *The Concept of Ideology and Other Essays* (New York: Vintage Books, 1967), p. 139.

8. See, for example, Hans J. Morgenthau, Introduction to *Ethics and United States Foreign Policy* by Ernest W. Lefever (New York: Meridian Books, 1957), pp. xv-xix; "Education and the World Scene," in *Education in the Age of Science*, ed. Brand Blandshard (New York: Basic Books, 1959), pp. 117–64; and especially "The Purpose of Political Science," in *A Design for Political Science: Scope, Objectives, and Methods*, ed. James C. Charlesworth (Philadelphia: American Academy of Political and Social Science, 1966), pp. 63–79.

9. Niebuhr and Morgenthau, "The Ethics of War and Peace in the Nuclear Age," p. 4.

10. Hans J. Morgenthau, *Scientific Man vs. Power Politics* (Chicago: University of Chicago Press, 1946), p. 168.

11. Ibid., p. 192.

12. Hans J. Morgenthau, *Science: Servant or Master?* (New York: New American Library, 1972).

13. Aristotle *Metaphysics* 1. 1–2. References to Aristotle are taken from *The Basic Works of Aristotle*, ed. Richard McKeon (New York: Random House, 1941).

14. Josef Pieper, *Leisure: The Basis of Culture* (New York: New American Library, 1963), p. 99.

15. Ibid., p. 100.

16. *Science: Servant or Master?*, p. 25.

17. Ibid., p. 27.

18. Ibid., pp. 26–27, 56–58. Morgenthau does not correctly understand what Socrates means in the *Phaedo* by describing philosophers as those who practice dying. For Socrates and Plato, *Thanatos* was a liberating force that did not hold the terror and futility it does for the bourgeois soul. The imminent prospect of death serves only to fortify the philosopher's life work to disengage the soul from temporal concerns, not to intensify, as it does for Morgenthau, a preoccupation with security and material weal. Socrates called those who fret because they are about to die *philosomas.*

19. Thomas Hobbes, *Leviathan* (1651; reprint ed., Oxford: Clarendon Press, 1947), chaps. 13–14.

20. *Science: Servant or Master?*, p. 27.

21. Ibid., p. 30.

22. Ibid., p. 31.

23. Ibid., p. 32. We are given an insight into Morgenthau's bourgeois spirit by his essay "Love and Power," in *The Restoration of American Politics*, vol. 3 of *Politics in the Twentieth Century* (Chicago: University of Chicago Press, 1962), pp. 7–14. One need not deny the insufficiency of man in isolation. For Morgenthau, however, love and power are two means by which man attempts to overcome his insufficiency, and the essential object of both is to duplicate his individuality. The lust for individuality and its unfettered expression was portrayed by Jacob Burckhardt in the irruption of the bourgeoisie during the Renaissance, and it has informed much of modern thought.

24. Eric Voegelin, *The New Science of Politics* (Chicago: University of Chicago Press, 1952), pp. 63–68.

25. Ibid., pp. 180–86.

26. Leo Strauss, *The Political Philosophy of Hobbes: Its Basis and Its Genesis* (Chicago: University of Chicago Press, 1952), pp. 100–101.

27. *Science: Servant or Master?*, pp. 35–45.

28. Ibid., p. 54.

29. Strauss, p. 161.

30. Ibid., p. 107.

31. See C. B. Macpherson, *The Political Theory of Possessive Individualism: Hobbes to Locke* (Oxford: Clarendon Press, 1962), especially pp. 70–106. Macpherson, a socialist, praises Hobbes for accomplishing certain things, though he believes we can and must now progress to socialism. Hobbes demystified political theory by repudiating natural law and revealing how truth is historical in nature. Moreover, his materialist conception of human nature and his amoral assignation of equal rights to equal appetites make Hobbes a precursor of scientific materialism. Macpherson argues that Hobbes succeeded in establishing the only kind of obligation possible in bourgeois society, but now different material conditions supply an alternative theory of moral and political obligation.

32. *Science: Servant or Master?*, p. 72.

33. Aristotle *Politics* 1; Plato *Republic* 2; St. Thomas Aquinas *Commentary on the Nicomachean Ethics* I, Lect. 1. For St. Thomas, of course, man's end extends beyond civil society, but his final supernatural end does not annihilate his temporal good;

however, this point is not at issue here. References to Plato are taken from *The Collected Dialogues of Plato Including the Letters*, eds. Edith Hamilton and Huntington Cairns (Princeton, N.J.: Princeton University Press, 1961). My use of St. Thomas's *Commentary on the Nicomachean Ethics* is based upon the translation by C. I. Litzinger, O. P. (Chicago: Henry Regnery Company, 1964).

34. Aristotle *Politics* 1267b5.

35. Ibid., 1324b30–1324b40.

36. St. Thomas Aquinas *Summa Theologica* I, Q.96, a.4. Unless otherwise specified, citations from Aquinas are taken from *Basic Writings of Saint Thomas Aquinas*, ed. Anton C. Pegis (New York: Random House, 1945).

37. St. Thomas Aquinas *Summa Theologica* I–II, Q.95, a.1.

38. *Scientific Man vs. Power Politics*, p. 203.

39. See, for example, Hans J. Morgenthau, "The Primacy of the National Interest," *American Scholar* 18 (Spring 1949): 207–12; "The Mainsprings of American Foreign Policy: The National Interest vs. Moral Abstractions," *American Political Science Review* 44 (December 1950): 833–54. The latter essay is reprinted in *In Defense of the National Interest: A Critical Examination of American Foreign Policy* (New York: Alfred A. Knopf, 1952). These seminal works apply Morgenthau's basic theory of politics to the practice of American foreign policy and explicate his central thesis of the realistic pursuit of national interest defined in terms of power.

40. Hans J. Morgenthau, *Politics among Nations: The Struggle for Power and Peace* (New York: Alfred A. Knopf, 1950), p. 17.

41. *Science: Servant or Master?*, p. 45.

42. St. Thomas Aquinas *Summa Theologica* I–II, Q.90, a. 1, ad3.

43. Aristotle *Nicomachean Ethics* 1140b5.

44. St. Thomas Aquinas *Summa Theologica* I–II, Q.57, a.5.

45. Josef Pieper, *Prudence* (New York: Pantheon Books, Inc., 1959), p. 18.

46. Ibid., pp. 21–22.

47. Quoted in ibid., p. 50.

48. Quoted in ibid.

49. Louis I. Bredvold and Ralph G. Ross, eds., *The Philosophy of Edmund Burke: A Selection from His Speeches and Writings* (Ann Arbor, Mich.: University of Michigan Press, 1967), p. 35.

50. Edmund Burke, *Reflections on the Revolution in France*, in *Reflections on the French Revolution*, intro. by A. J. Grieve (London: J. M. Dent & Sons, Ltd., 1955), p. 6.

51. *Scientific Man vs. Power Politics*, p. 13.

52. Ibid., pp. 122–23.

53. Ibid., pp. 157–58.

54. Ibid., p. 203.

55. Ibid., pp. 219–20.

56. *Science: Servant or Master?*, p. 45.

57. See Hans J. Morgenthau, "Another 'Great Debate': The National Interest of the United States," *American Political Science Review* 46 (December 1952): 961–88. Morgenthau denies he is a Hobbesian and claims to offer five ways moral principles

apply to state action. Actually, he does nothing of the sort, even in the most general fashion, and succeeds only in demonstrating how marginal to his mind this connection is. Cf. "The Problem of the National Interest," in *Dilemmas of Politics* (Chicago: University of Chicago Press, 1958), pp. 54–87.

58. Morgenthau, "The Perils of Empiricism," in *The Restoration of American Politics*, pp. 109–16.

59. Morgenthau, "A Positive Approach to a Democratic Ideology," in *The Restoration of American Politics*, pp. 237–47.

60. Karl Marx and Friedrich Engels, "Manifesto of the Communist Party," in *The Marx-Engels Reader*, ed. Robert C. Tucker (New York: W. W. Norton & Company, 1972), p. 339.

61. See, for example, Hans J. Morgenthau, *The Decline of Democratic Politics*, vol. 1 of *Politics in the Twentieth Century* (Chicago: University of Chicago Press, 1962), pp. 7–15, 127–30, 220–26.

62. Hans J. Morgenthau, "The Machiavellian Utopia," *Ethics* 55 (January 1945): 147.

63. Morgenthau, "The Commitments of a Theory of International Politics," in *Dilemmas of Politics*, p. 52.

64. Morgenthau, "International Law," in *Dilemmas of Politics*, p. 218.

65. Ibid., p. 224.

66. Morgenthau, *Politics among Nations: The Struggle for Power and Peace*, pp. 172–73.

67. Plato *Republic* 338c.

68. Thucydides *The Peloponnesian War* (trans. Thomas Hobbes) 5.89.

69. Morgenthau, "Naziism," in *The Decline of Democratic Politics*, pp. 227–40.

70. Morgenthau, "The Tragedy of German–Jewish Liberalism," in *The Decline of Democratic Politics*, pp. 247–56.

71. Morgenthau, "National Socialist Doctrine of World Organization," in *The Decline of Democratic Politics*, pp. 245–46.

72. Morgenthau, "Christian Ethics and Political Action," in *The Decline of Democratic Politics*, pp. 375–76.

73. Morgenthau, "The Demands of Prudence," in *The Restoration of American Politics*, p. 15. See also "The Evil of Politics and the Ethics of Evil," *Ethics* 56 (October 1945): 1–18; and "The Moral Dilemma of Political Action," in *Dilemmas of Politics*, pp. 246–55.

74. Morgenthau, Introduction to *Ethics and United States Foreign Policy*, p. xviii.

75. Morgenthau, "The Revival of Objective Standards: Walter Lippmann," in *Dilemmas of Politics*, pp. 377–81.

76. See, for example, Morgenthau, "Education and the World Scene," and "The Purpose of Political Science." At times Morgenthau certainly sounds the high moralist, as in his suggestively entitled "Epistle to the Columbians on the Meaning of Morality," reprinted in *The Purpose of American Politics* (New York: Alfred A. Knopf, 1960), pp. 351–59.

77. Hans J. Morgenthau, "The Influence of Reinhold Niebuhr in American Political Life and Thought," in *Reinhold Niebuhr: A Prophetic Voice in Our Time*, ed. Harold R. Landon (Greenwich, N.Y.: Seabury Press, 1962), p. 109.

78. Reinhold Niebuhr, untitled response in *Reinhold Niebuhr: A Prophetic Voice in Our Time*, p. 122.

79. Niccolò Machiavelli, *The Prince*, intro. by Max Lerner (New York: Random House, 1950), p. 156.

80. Morgenthau, *The Purpose of American Politics*, p. 8.

81. Ibid., p. 21.

82. Ibid., p. 54.

83. Ibid., p. 31.

84. Ibid., pp. 143–96.

85. Ibid., p. 238.

86. Cf. Plato *Republic* 8.

87. Morgenthau, *The Purpose of American Politics*, pp. 266 ff.

88. See John Adams, "A Defence of the Constitutions of Government of the United States of America" and "Discourses on Davila," in *The Works of John Adams . . .*, ed. Charles Francis Adams, 10 vols. (Boston: Little, Brown and Company, 1850–56), vols. 4–6.

89. Edmund Burke, "Letter to a Member of the National Assembly, in Answer to Some Objections to His Book on French Affairs," in *Reflections on the French Revolution*, pp. 281–82.

90. Morgenthau, *The Purpose of American Politics*, pp. 297–98.

91. See *The Federalist Papers*, ed. Clinton Rossiter (New York: The New American Library, 1961), especially #10 and #51. The great problem addressed in *Federalist* #10 is how to check factions that arise from the passions and interests of men. Madison decided that the optimal solution was to control the effects of faction, rather than eliminate their cause, liberty, for the unequal abilities of men inevitably give rise to unequal property, and this is the main root of faction. Consequently, the protection of unequal faculties, and hence unequal property, constitutes the principal purpose of government. What Madison implied was that since the inexpungeable pride and self-interest of man wholly vitiate his reason, the task of politics is to play one competing appetite off against another; moreover, this purpose will be enhanced by expanding and multiplying the various, antagonistic lusts of men. Madison realized that all political theory is based upon a conception of human nature, and *Federalist* #51, which is devoted to the separation of powers in government, is likewise based upon the countervailing balance of private lusts as the work of prudence.

92. See Morgenthau, *The Purpose of American Politics*, pp. 293–323, and *Dilemmas of Politics*, pp. 104–22. In an article entitled "Comment on Morgenthau's 'Dilemmas of Freedom,'" *American Political Science Review* 51 (September 1957): 724–33, Howard B. White ably demonstrates the cul-de-sac to which Morgenthau's relativism leads. I want to suggest here the frightful, universal implications of this predicament.

93. Hans J. Morgenthau, "The American Political Legacy," in *Theory and Practice in American Politics*, ed. William H. Nelson (Chicago: University of Chicago Press, 1964), p. 149.

94. Aristotle *Politics* 1310a25–1310a35.

95. Morgenthau, "The Decline of Democratic Government," in *Dilemmas of Politics*, p. 286.

96. Ibid.

97. See, for example, Morgenthau, *Truth and Power*, pp. 3–9, 13–28, 29–39, 40–44.

98. Ibid., p. 65.

99. Ibid., p. 62.

100. F. Scott Fitzgerald, *The Great Gatsby* (New York: Charles Scribner's Sons, 1925), p. 182.

Notes to Epilogue

1. White, *Social Thought in America*, p. x.

2. Sidney Hook, "The New Failure of Nerve," *Partisan Review* 10 (January-February 1943):16, 9.

3. Reinhold Niebuhr, *Man's Nature and His Communities: Essays on the Dynamics and Enigmas of Man's Personal and Social Existence* (New York: Charles Scribner's Sons, 1965), p. 23.

4. White, *Social Thought in America*, p. 256.

5. Sidney Hook, *Heresy, Yes—Conspiracy, No!* (New York: The American Committee for Cultural Freedom, 1952), p. 3.

6. White, *Social Thought in America*, p. 257.

7. Ibid., p. 266.

8. See ibid., pp. 265–66, 272–74.

9. St. Thomas Aquinas *Commentary on the Nicomachean Ethics* I, Lect. 3.

10. St. Thomas Aquinas *Summa Theologica* I-II, Q.94, a.2.

11. Ibid.

12. St. Thomas Aquinas *Summa Theologica* I–II, Q.94, a.4–5.

13. Ibid., Q.95, a.2, ad 3.

14. White, *Social Thought in America*, p. 275.

15. St. Thomas Aquinas *Summa Theologica* II–II, Q.57, a.2. This passage is taken from Dino Bigongiari, ed., *The Political Ideas of St. Thomas Aquinas* (New York: Hafner Publishing Company, 1969).

16. St. Thomas Aquinas *Commentary on the Nicomachean Ethics* V, Lect. 12.

17. Ibid.

18. St. Thomas Aquinas *Summa Theologica* II-II, Q.57, a.3.

19. See Walter Lippmann, *Essays in the Public Philosophy* (Boston: Little, Brown and Company, 1955), pp. 152–59.

20. White, *Social Thought in America*, p. 237.

21. Ibid., p. 243.

22. Ibid.

23. Ibid., p. 244.

24. Ibid.

25. Ibid., p. 245.

26. Ibid., p. 256.

27. For an elaboration of his position the reader may wish to refer to White's *Toward Reunion in Philosophy* (New York: Atheneum, 1963), esp. pp. 279–99. White acknowledges that we possess certain moral beliefs, which he variously terms *a priori*, *pinned-down*, or *terminal*. The source of these principles is merely our firm belief; they are not fixed, nor is their truth established by any universal meaning or objective quality and relation. He suggests that a descriptive statement of fact may coincide with a statement of value, but he insists that moral principles are indistinguishable from their "singular conclusions in their mode of justification" (p. 286). In judging the morality of a political action our answer is obtained by estimating the consequences of performing such an action or of adopting an alternative. White admits departing from a pure pragmatism in that he would allow more than the capacity to predict experience—for example, respect for older beliefs, simplicity, clarity, etcetera—as the test of the truth of an idea. William James, of course, had conceded as much, but White thinks that to do so is to go beyond pragmatism in a strict sense. White denies, however, that there is any principle for selecting our moral beliefs, or that there is any definition of the rightness of an action.

28. Quoted in White, *Social Thought in America*, p. 278.

29. Ibid., p. 254.

Bibliography

Adams, John. *The Works of John Adams* . . . Edited by Charles Francis Adams. 10 vols. Boston: Little, Brown and Company, 1850–56.

Aquinas, Saint Thomas. *Basic Writings of Saint Thomas Aquinas.* Edited by Anton C. Pegis. 2 vols. New York: Random House, 1945.

————. *Commentary on the Nicomachean Ethics.* Translated by C. I. Litzinger. O.P. Chicago: Henry Regnery Co., 1964.

————. *The Political Ideas of St. Thomas Aquinas.* Edited by Dino Bigongiari. New York: Hafner Publishing Co., 1969.

Aristotle. *The Basic Works of Aristotle.* Edited by Richard McKeon. New York: Random House, 1941.

Bell, Daniel. *The End of Ideology: On the Exhaustion of Political Ideas in the Fifties.* Rev. ed. New York: Free Press, 1962.

Benda, Julien. *The Treason of the Intellectuals.* Translated by Richard Aldington. New York: W. W. Norton and Co., 1969.

Bernstein, Barton J. "American Foreign Policy and the Origins of the Cold War." *Politics and Policies of the Truman Administration.* Edited by Barton J. Bernstein. Chicago: Quadrangle Books, 1970.

Bourne, Randolph S. *War and the Intellectuals: Essays by Randolph S. Bourne, 1915–1919.* Edited by Carl Resek. New York: Harper and Row, 1964.

Brandon, Donald. *American Foreign Policy: Beyond Utopianism and Realism.* New York: Appleton-Century-Crofts, 1966.

Burke, Edmund. "Letter to a Member of the National Assembly, in Answer to Some Objections to His Book on French Affairs." *Reflections on the French Revolution.* Introduction by A. J. Grieve. London: J. M. Dent & Sons, Ltd., 1955.

_____. *The Philosophy of Edmund Burke: A Selection from His Speeches and Writings.* Edited by Louis I. Bredvold and Ralph G. Ross. Ann Arbor, Mich.: University of Michigan Press, Ann Arbor Paperbacks, 1967.

_____. *Reflections on the Revolution in France. Reflections on the French Revolution.* Introduction by A. J. Grieve. London: J. M. Dent & Sons, Ltd., 1955.

Butterfield, Herbert. *Christianity, Diplomacy and War.* London: Epworth Press, 1953.

Childress, James F. "Reinhold Niebuhr's Critique of Pacifism." *Review of Politics* 36 (October 1974): 467–91.

Claude, Inis L., Jr. *Power and International Relations.* New York: Random House, 1962.

Cook, Thomas I., and Moos, Malcolm. "Foreign Policy: The Realism of Idealism." *American Political Science Review* 46 (June 1952): 343–56.

Dunne, John S., C.S.C. "Realpolitik in the Decline of the West." *Review of Politics* 21 (January 1959): 131–50.

Eliot, T. S. *Christianity and Culture: The Idea of a Christian Society and Notes towards the Definition of Culture.* New York: Harcourt, Brace and World, 1949.

Gaddis, John Lewis. *The United States and the Origins of the Cold War: 1941–1947.* New York: Columbia University Press, 1972.

Galbraith, John Kenneth. *American Capitalism: The Concept of Countervailing Power.* 2d ed. rev. Boston: Houghton Mifflin Co., 1956.

Gardner, Lloyd C. *Architects of Illusion: Men and Ideas in American Foreign Policy, 1941–1949.* Chicago: Quadrangle Books, 1970.

Geiger, George R. "Retreat to What?" *Antioch Review* 6 (December 1946): 625–27.

Good, Robert C. "The National Interest and Political Realism: Niebuhr's 'Debate' with Morgenthau and Kennan." *Journal of Politics* 22 (November 1960): 597–619.

Halle, Louis J. "George Kennan and the Common Mind." *Virginia Quarterly Review* 45 (Winter 1969): 46–57.

———. "The World of George Kennan." *New Republic,* August 7, 1961, pp. 21–23.

Hamilton, Alexander; Madison, James; and Jay, John. *The Federalist Papers.* Edited by Clinton Rossiter. New York: New American Library, Mentor Books, 1961.

Harland, Gordon. *The Thought of Reinhold Niebuhr.* New York: Oxford University Press, 1960.

Hermens, Ferdinand A. "Ethics, Politics, and Power: Christian Realism and Manichaean Dualism." *Ethics* 68 (July 1958): 246–59.

Herz, John H. *Political Realism and Political Idealism.* Chicago: University of Chicago Press, 1951.

Hobbes, Thomas. *Leviathan.* 1651. Reprint. Oxford: Clarendon Press, 1947.

Hoffmann, Stanley H. "International Relations: The Long Road to Theory." *World Politics* 11 (April 1959): 346–77.

Hook, Sidney. *Heresy, Yes—Conspiracy, No!* New York: The American Committee for Cultural Freedom, 1952.

———. "The New Failure of Nerve." *Partisan Review* 10 (January-February 1943): 2–23.

Howell, Ronald F. "Political Philosophy on a Theological Foundation: An Expository Analysis of the Political Thought of Reinhold Niebuhr." *Ethics* 63 (January 1953): 79–99.

Kateb, George. "George F. Kennan: The Heart of a Diplomat." *Commentary,* January, 1968, pp. 21–26.

Kegley, Charles W., and Bretall, Robert W., eds. *Reinhold Niebuhr: His Religious, Social and Political Thought.* New York: Macmillan Co., 1956.

Kennan, George F. *American Diplomacy: 1900–1950.* Chicago: University of Chicago Press, 1951.

———."Communism and Conformity." *Bulletin of the Atomic Scientists* 9 (October 1953): p. 296.

———. "Current Problems in the Conduct of Foreign Policy." *Department of State Bulletin,* May 15, 1950, p. 747.

————. "Disengagement Revisited." *Foreign Affairs* 37 (January 1959): 187–210.

————. "The Evolution of the U.S.S.R." *World Technology and Human Destiny*. Edited by Raymond Aron. Ann Arbor, Mich.: University of Michigan Press, 1963.

————. "Foreign Policy and the Christian Conscience." *Atlantic Monthly*, May, 1959, pp. 44–49.

————. *From Prague after Munich: Diplomatic Papers, 1938–1940*. Princeton, N.J.: Princeton University Press, 1968.

————. "The Future of Our Professional Diplomacy." *Foreign Affairs* 33 (July 1955): 566–86.

————. "History and Diplomacy as Viewed by a Diplomatist." *Review of Politics* 18 (April 1956): 170–77.

————. "How Stands Our Pursuit of Happiness?" *New Leader*, June 20, 1955, pp. 16–18.

————. "The International Situation." *Department of State Bulletin*, September 5, 1949, pp. 323–24.

————. "Let Peace Not Die of Neglect." *New York Times Magazine*, February 25, 1951, p. 10.

————. *Memoirs: 1925–1950*. Boston: Little, Brown and Co., 1967.

————. *Memoirs: 1950–1963*. Boston: Little, Brown and Co., 1972.

————. "The Nature of the Challenge." *New Republic*, August 24, 1953, pp. 9–12.

————. *On Dealing with the Communist World*. New York: Harper and Row, 1964.

————. "Overdue Changes in Our Foreign Policy." *Harper's Magazine*, August, 1956, pp. 27–33.

————. "Peaceful Coexistence: A Western View." *Foreign Affairs* 38 (January 1960): 171–90.

————. "Philosophy and Strategy in America's Postwar Policy." A lecture delivered at the Graduate Institute of International Studies, Geneva, May 11, 1965.

————. *Realities of American Foreign Policy*. Princeton, N.J.: Princeton University Press, 1954.

————. "Renaissance of Philosophy?" *World Technology and Human Destiny*. Edited by Raymond Aron. Ann Arbor, Mich.: University of Michigan Press, 1963.

————. *Russia and the United States.* Stamford, Conn.: Overbrook Press, 1950.

————. *Russia and the West under Lenin and Stalin.* Boston: Little, Brown and Company, 1961.

————. *Russia, the Atom, and the West.* New York: Harper and Brothers, 1958.

————. "The Russian Revolution—Fifty Years After: Its Nature and Consequences." *Foreign Affairs* 46 (October 1967): 1–21.

————. "Soviet-American Relations: General Principles on Which to Base Policy." *Vital Speeches of the Day,* February 15, 1953, pp. 268–72.

————. *Soviet Foreign Policy: 1917–1941.* Princeton, N.J.: D. Van Nostrand Co., 1960.

————. "The Soviet Will Never Recover." *Saturday Evening Post,* November 24, 1956, p. 32.

————. "Speak Truth to Power—A Reply by George Kennan." *Progressive* 19 (October 1955): 16–18.

————. "The 'Third World' and the Industrial Society." *World Technology and Human Destiny.* Edited by Raymond Aron. Ann Arbor, Mich.: University of Michigan Press, 1963.

————. "Training for Statesmanship." *Atlantic Monthly,* May, 1953, pp. 40–43.

————. "Where Do You Stand on Communism?" *New York Times Magazine,* May 27, 1951, p. 7.

Kolko, Gabriel. *The Politics of War: The World and United States Foreign Policy, 1943–1945.* New York: Random House, 1968.

LaFeber, Walter. *America, Russia, and the Cold War: 1945–1966.* New York: John Wiley and Sons, 1967.

Landon, Harold R., ed. *Reinhold Niebuhr: A Prophetic Voice in Our Time.* Greenwich, N.Y.: Seabury Press, 1962.

Lasch, Christopher. "The Historian as Diplomat." *Nation,* November 24, 1962, pp. 348–53.

Lichtheim, George. *The Concept of Ideology and Other Essays.* New York: Alfred A. Knopf and Random House, Vintage Books, 1967.

Lippmann, Walter. *The Cold War: A Study in U.S. Foreign Policy.* New York: Harper and Brothers, 1947.

————. *Essays in the Public Philosophy*. Boston: Little, Brown and Company, 1955.

Lipset, Seymour Martin. *Political Man: The Social Bases of Politics*. New York: Doubleday and Co., 1960.

McDougal, Myres S. "Law and Power." *American Journal of International Law* 46 (January 1952): 102–14.

Machiavelli, Niccolò. *The Prince*. Introduction by Max Lerner. New York: Random House, Modern Library, 1950.

Macpherson, C. B. *The Political Theory of Possessive Individualism: Hobbes to Locke*. Oxford: Clarendon Press, 1962.

McWilliams, Wilson Carey. "Reinhold Niebuhr: New Orthodoxy for an Old Liberalism." *American Political Science Review* 56 (December 1962): 874–85.

Maier, Charles S. "Revisionism and the Interpretation of Cold War Origins." *Perspectives in American History*, no. 4 (1970), pp. 313–47.

Maritain, Jacques. *True Humanism*. Translated by M. R. Adamson. 4th ed. rev. London: Geoffrey Bles, Centenary Press, 1946.

Marx, Karl, and Engels, Friedrich. "Manifesto of the Communist Party," *The Marx-Engels Reader*. Edited by Robert C. Tucker New York: W. W. Norton & Company, 1972.

May, Henry F. *Protestant Churches and Industrial America*. New York: Octagon Books, 1963.

Meyer, Donald B. *The Protestant Search for Political Realism: 1919–1941*. Berkeley, Calif.: University of California Press, 1960.

Morgenthau, Hans J. "The American Political Legacy." *Theory and Practice in American Politics*. Edited by William H. Nelson. Chicago: University of Chicago Press, 1964.

————. "Another 'Great Debate': The National Interest of the United States." *American Political Science Review* 46 (December 1952): 961–88.

————. *Dilemmas of Politics*. Chicago: University of Chicago Press, 1958.

————. "Education and the World Scene." *Education in the Age of Science*. Edited by Brand Blanshard. New York: Harper and Row, Basic Books, 1959.

————. "The Evil of Politics and the Ethics of Evil." *Ethics* 56 (October 1945): 1–18.

_____. *In Defense of the National Interest: A Critical Examination of American Foreign Policy.* New York: Alfred A. Knopf, 1952.

_____. Introduction to *Ethics and United States Foreign Policy,* by Ernest W. Lefever. Cleveland and New York: World Publishing Company, Meridian Books, 1957.

_____. "The Machiavellian Utopia." *Ethics* 55 (January 1945): 145–47.

_____. *Politics among Nations: The Struggle for Power and Peace.* New York: Alfred A. Knopf, 1950.

_____. *Politics in the Twentieth Century.* 3 vols. Chicago: University of Chicago Press, 1962.

_____. "The Primacy of the National Interest." *American Scholar* 18 (Spring 1949): 207–12.

_____. *The Purpose of American Politics.* New York: Alfred A. Knopf, 1960.

_____. "The Purpose of Political Science." *A Design for Political Science: Scope, Objectives, and Methods.* Edited by James C. Charlesworth. Philadelphia: American Academy of Political and Social Science, 1966.

_____. *Science: Servant or Master?* New York: New American Library, 1972.

_____. *Scientific Man vs. Power Politics.* Chicago: University of Chicago Press, 1946.

_____. *Truth and Power: Essays of a Decade, 1960–70.* New York: Praeger, 1970.

Murray, John Courtney, S. J. *We Hold These Truths: Catholic Reflections on the American Proposition.* New York: Sheed and Ward, 1960.

Niebuhr, Reinhold. "Alternatives to the H-Bomb." *New Leader,* August 2, 1954, pp. 12–14.

_____. "America and the Asians." *New Leader,* May 31, 1954, pp. 3–4.

_____. "American Conservatism and the World Crisis: A Study in Vacillation." *Yale Review* 40 (March 1951): 385-99.

_____. "American Pride and Power." *American Scholar* 17 (Autumn 1948): 393–94.

————. "America's Precarious Eminence." *Virginia Quarterly Review* 23 (Autumn 1947): 481–90.

————. "The Anatomy of American Nationalism." *New Leader,* February 28, 1955, pp. 16–17.

————. "Anglo-Saxon Tensions." *Spectator,* February 16, 1945, pp. 142–43.

————. "The Anomaly of European Socialism." *Yale Review* 42 (December 1952): 161–67.

————. *Beyond Tragedy: Essays on the Christian Interpretation of History.* New York: Charles Scribner's Sons, 1937.

————. "Can We Avoid Catastrophe?" *Christian Century,* May 26, 1948, pp. 504–6.

————. "The Case for Coexistence." *New Leader,* October 4, 1954, pp. 5–6.

————. "The Change in Russia." *New Leader,* October 3, 1955, pp. 18–19.

————. *The Children of Light and the Children of Darkness: A Vindication of Democracy and a Critique of Its Traditional Defense.* New York: Charles Scribner's Sons, 1944.

————. "Christian Faith and Social Action." *Christian Faith and Social Action.* Edited by John A. Hutchinson. New York: Charles Scribner's Sons, 1953.

————. "The Christian Faith and the Economic Life of Liberal Society." *Goals of Economic Life.* Edited by A. Dudley Ward. New York: Harper and Brothers. 1953.

————. *Christian Realism and Political Problems.* New York: Charles Scribner's Sons, 1953.

————. "Christianity and Communism: Social Justice." *Spectator,* November 6, 1936, pp. 802–3.

————. *Christianity and Power Politics.* New York: Charles Scribner's Sons, 1952.

————. "Coercion, Self-Interest, and Love." *The Organizational Revolution: A Study in the Ethics of Economic Organization.* Edited by Kenneth E. Boulding. New York: Harper and Brothers, 1953.

————. "Co-Existence or Total War." *Christian Century,* August 18, 1954, pp. 971–73.

————. "Communism and the Clergy." *Christian Century,* August 19, 1953, pp. 936–37.

————. "The Conditions of Our Survival." *Virginia Quarterly Review* 26 (Autumn 1950): 481–91.

————. "Democracy and the Party Spirit." *New Leader,* March 15, 1954, pp. 3–5.

————. "Democratic Goals and World Order." *New Leader,* September 23, 1944, pp. 4–5.

————. "Europe, Russia, and America." *Nation,* September 14, 1946, pp. 288–89.

————. "The Evil of the Communist Idea." *New Leader,* June 8, 1953, pp. 16–18.

————. "Factors of Cohesion." *Spectator,* June 18, 1943, pp. 562–63.

————. "The Fate of European Socialism." *New Leader,* June 20, 1955, pp. 6–8.

————. "The Fight for Germany." *Life,* October 21, 1946, pp. 65–72.

————. "Fighting Chance for a Sick Society." *Nation,* March 22, 1941, pp. 357–60.

————. "For Peace, We Must Risk War." *Life,* September 20, 1948, pp. 38–39.

————. "Great Britain's Post-War Role." *Nation,* July 10, 1943, pp. 39–40.

————. "Halfway to What?" *Nation,* January 14, 1950, pp. 26–28.

————. "Hazards and Resources." *Virginia Quarterly Review* 25 (Spring 1949): 194–205.

————. "Ideology and Pretense." *Nation,* December 9, 1939, pp. 645–46.

————. "The Illusion of World Government." *Foreign Affairs* 27 (April 1949): 379–88.

————. *The Irony of American History.* New York: Charles Scribner's Sons, 1952.

————. "Is This 'Peace in Our Time'?" *Nation,* April 7, 1945, pp. 382–84.

————. "Leaves from the Notebook of a War-Bound American." *Christian Century,* October 25, 1939, pp. 1298–99; November 15, 1939, pp. 1405–6; December 6, 1939, pp. 1502–3.

————. "Liberalism: Illusions and Realities." *New Republic,* July 4, 1955, pp. 11–13.

————. "The Limits of Military Power." *New Leader,* May 30, 1955, pp. 16–17.

————. *Man's Nature and His Communities: Essays on the Dynamics and Enigmas of Man's Personal and Social Existence.* New York: Charles Scribner's Sons, 1965.

————. "Marxism in Eclipse." *Spectator,* June 4, 1943, pp. 518–19.

————. "The Meaning of Labor Unity." *New Leader,* March 28, 1955, pp. 8–9.

————. "The Moral Implications of Loyalty to the United Nations." *The Hazen Pamphlets,* no. 29. New Haven, Conn.: Edward W. Hazen Foundation, Inc., 1952.

————. *Moral Man and Immoral Society: A Study in Ethics and Politics.* New York: Charles Scribner's Sons, 1934.

————. *The Nature and Destiny of Man: A Christian Interpretation.* 2 vols. New York: Charles Scribner's Sons, 1947.

————. "New Allies, Old Issues." *Nation,* July 19, 1941, pp. 50–52.

————. "Our Country and Our Culture: A Symposium." *Partisan Review* 19 (May-June 1952): 301–3.

————. "Our Relations to Russia." *Toward a Better World.* Edited by William Scarlett. Philadelphia: John C. Winston Co., 1946.

————. "The Pathos of Liberalism." *Nation,* September 11, 1935, pp. 303–4.

————. "Peace and the Liberal Illusion." *Nation,* January 28, 1939, pp. 117–19.

————. "The Pillars of Peace." *Spectator,* October 22, 1943, pp. 378–79.

————. "The Problem of a Protestant Social Ethic." *Union Seminary Quarterly Review* 15 (November 1959): 1–11.

————. "A Protest against a Dilemma's Two Horns." *World Politics* 2 (April 1950): 338–44.

————. "Russia and Karl Marx." *Nation,* May 7, 1938, pp. 530–31.

————. "Russia and the Communist Party." *Nation,* April 10, 1943, p. 537.

_____. "Russia and the West." *Nation,* January 16, 1943, pp. 82–84; January 23, 1943, pp. 124–25.

_____. *The Self and the Dramas of History.* New York: Charles Scribner's Sons, 1955.

_____. *The Structure of Nations and Empires.* New York: Charles Scribner's Sons, 1959.

_____. "Ten Years That Shook My World." *Christian Century,* April 26, 1939, pp. 542–46.

_____. "They All Fear America." *Christian Century,* August 20, 1947, pp. 993-94.

_____. "To Prevent the Triumph of an Intolerable Tyranny." *Christian Century,* December 18, 1940, pp. 1578-80.

_____. "Transatlantic Tension." *Reporter,* September 18, 1951, pp. 14-16.

_____. "Why They Dislike America." *New Leader,* April 12, 1954, pp. 3-5.

_____."Will America Back Out?" *Nation,* January 13, 1945, pp. 42-43.

_____, and Morgenthau, Hans J. "The Ethics of War and Peace in the Nuclear Age." *War/Peace Report* 7 (February 1967): 3-8.

O'Connor, Edward D., C.S.C. "The Theology of Reinhold Niebuhr." *Review of Politics* 23 (April 1961): 172-202.

Pieper, Josef. *Leisure: The Basis of Culture.* Translated by Alexander Dru. New York: New American Library, Mentor-Omega Books, 1963.

_____. *Prudence.* New York: Pantheon Books, 1959.

Plato. *The Collected Dialogues of Plato Including the Letters.* Edited by Edith Hamilton and Huntington Cairns. Bollingen Series, no. 71. Princeton, N.J.: Princeton University Press, 1961.

Rhoades, Dan. "The Prophetic Insight and Theoretical-Analytical Inadequacy of 'Christian Realism.' " *Ethics* 75 (October 1964): 1-15.

Schilling, Warner R. "The Clarification of Ends or, Which Interest Is the National?" *World Politics* 8 (July 1956): 566-78.

Schlesinger, Arthur M., Jr. "Origins of the Cold War." *Twentieth-Century America: Recent Interpretations.* Edited by Barton J.

Bernstein and Allen J. Matusow. New York: Harcourt, Brace and World, 1969.

————. *The Vital Center: The Politics of Freedom.* Boston: Houghton Mifflin Co., 1949.

Scott, Nathan A., Jr., ed. *The Legacy of Reinhold Niebuhr.* Chicago: University of Chicago Press, 1975.

Steel, Ronald. *Imperialists and Other Heroes: A Chronicle of the American Empire.* New York: Random House, 1971.

————. "Man without a Country." *New York Review of Books,* January 4, 1968, pp. 8–15.

Stone, Ronald. *Reinhold Niebuhr: Prophet to Politicians.* Nashville, Tenn.: Abingdon Press, 1972.

Strauss, Leo. *The Political Philosophy of Hobbes: Its Basis and Its Genesis.* Chicago: University of Chicago Press, 1952.

Sturm, Douglas. "A Critique of American Protestant Social and Political Thought." *Journal of Politics* 26 (November 1964): 896-913.

Tannenbaum, Frank. "The Balance of Power Versus the Coordinate State." *Political Science Quarterly* 67 (June 1952): 173-97.

Thompson, Kenneth W. "Beyond National Interest: A Critical Evaluation of Reinhold Niebuhr's Theory of International Politics." *Review of Politics* 17 (April 1955): 167-88.

Thucydides. *The Peloponnesian War.* Translated by Thomas Hobbes. 2 vols. Ann Arbor, Mich.: University of Michigan Press, 1959.

Tucker, Robert W. "Political Realism and Foreign Policy." *World Politics* 13 (April 1961): 461-70.

————. "Professor Morgenthau's Theory of Political 'Realism.' " *American Political Science Review* 46 (March 1952): 214-24.

————. *The Radical Left and American Foreign Policy.* Baltimore: Johns Hopkins Press, 1971.

United States. *Foreign Relations of the United States: Diplomatic Papers, 1945.* Vol. 5. *Europe.* Washington: U.S. Government Printing Office, 1965.

Voegelin, Eric. *The New Science of Politics.* Chicago: University of Chicago Press, 1952.

White, Howard B. "Comment on Morgenthau's 'Dilemmas of Freedom.'" *American Political Science Review* 51 (September 1957): 724-33.

White, Morton. *Social Thought in America: The Revolt against Formalism.* 2d ed. rev. Boston: Beacon Press, 1957.

_____. *Toward Reunion in Philosophy.* New York: Atheneum, 1963.

Williams, William Appleman. "The Irony of Containment: A Policy Boomerangs." *Nation*, May 5, 1956 pp. 376-79.

_____. *The Tragedy of American Diplomacy.* Rev. ed. New York: Delta Publishing Co., 1962.

Wolfers, Arnold. "Statesmanship and Moral Choice." *World Politics* 1 (January 1949): 175-95.

The following journals, while not read in their entirety for the years indicated, were of sufficient importance to warrant close examination. For individual citations, the reader may refer to the footnotes.

Christianity and Crisis. 1941-1954.

Christianity and Society. 1940-1956.

Radical Religion. 1935-1940.

INDEX

207